Your Ultimate Guide to Unlocking your Full Drumming Potential

BEGINNER TO ADVANCED COMPLETE SYLLABUS

THE DRUM HUB

Your Ultimate Guide to Unlocking your Full Drumming Potential

Copyright © 2025 by Joel Hammond and The Drum Hub. All rights reserved.

First Published 2025 by: Joel Hammond
Perth, Australia
www.thedrumhub.com.au

First Edition printed March 2025.

Notice of Rights
This book is sold subject to the condition that it shall not, by way of trade or otherwise, be lent, resold, hired out, or otherwise circulated without the publisher's prior consent, in any form of binding or cover, other than that in which it is published, and without a similar condition, including this condition being imposed on the subsequent purchaser. All rights reserved by the publisher. No part of this publication may be reproduced, stored in a retrieval system, or transmitted in any form, or by any means, electronic, digital, mechanical, photocopying, scanning, recorded or otherwise, without the prior written permission of the copyright owner. Requests to the copyright owner should be addressed to https://thedrumhub.com.au

Limits of Liability/Disclaimer of Warranty:
While the publisher and author have used their best efforts in preparing this book, they make no representations or warranties with respect to the accuracy or completeness of the contents of this book and specifically disclaim any implied warranties of merchantability or fitness for a particular purpose. No warranty may be created or extended by sales representatives or written sales materials. The advice and strategies contained herein may not be suitable for your situation. You should consult with a professional where appropriate. The intent of the author is only to offer information for a general nature. Neither the publisher nor author shall be liable for any loss of profit or any other commercial damages, including but not limited to special, incidental, consequential, or other damages. The author and the publisher assume no responsibility for your actions.

Where photographic images have been provided by the author and people are depicted, such images are being used for illustrative purposes only. Product names may be trademarks or registered trademarks, and are used for identification and explanation without intent to infringe.

National Library of Australia Cataloguing-in-Publication entry:
Author: Hammond, Joel
The Drum Hub / by Joel Hammond
ISBN 9780646714691 (Paperback)

Printed by Lightning Source
Typeset & cover design by Liz Atherton

ISBN: 978-0-646-71469-1

Your Ultimate Guide to Unlocking your Full Drumming Potential

BEGINNER TO ADVANCED COMPLETE SYLLABUS

TABLE OF CONTENTS

INTRODUCTION	
DRUM KIT APPENDIX	01
CORRECT STICK PLACEMENT AND POSTURE	02
CHAPTER 1	**03**
Note Scale	04
Staff lines and meanings	05
Dynamic terms and meanings	06
Whole note, Half note and Quarter note and Rest explanation	07
Repeats sign and 1st and 2nd endings explained	08
Understanding Da Capo, Del Segno, and D.S. al Fine	09
and Coda	09
Whole note Half notes Rest	10
quarter note and qtr note rest	11
quarter note foot and rest exeRcise	12
whole half quarter mixed note study	13
mixed note and rest combination study, part#1	14
Quarter note Rhythms 4/4 rock beat	15
quarter note rhythm with rolls and rest	16
mixed quarter note tom rolls	17
Skill tester #1	18
Solo exercise Part #1	19
student Practical summary	20
CHAPTER 2	**21**
understanding the 8th note	22
Quarters and 8th snare exercises	23
Quarters and 8th with foot exercises	24
understand the 8th note rest	25
quarter and 8th snare exercise with rests	26
quarter and 8th note rest with foot	27
High Hat and foot separation excercises	28
quarter and 8th note rest with foot	29
8th note rhythms	30
8th note accents	31
8th note accents on toms	32
8th note rhythms with quarter and 8th rolls	33
mixed note combinations on toms	34
quarter and 8th note combination study	35
quarter and 8th note transistions	36
syncopation part #1	37
8th note syncopated snare rhythms	38
8th note off beat rhythms	39
8th note high hat exercises	40
8th note high hat exercises	40
Skill Tester #2	41
solo exercise	42
Student Practical summary	43
CHAPTER 3	**44**
understanding the 16th note	45
quarter 16th on snare	46

8TH 16TH ON SNARE	47
16TH NOTE ACCENTS	48
QUARTER 8TH 16TH ON SNARE WITH FOOT	49
UNDERSTANDING THE 16 NOTE REST	50
MIXED NOTES AND REST CHALLENGE	51
16TH NOTE RHYTHMS WITH SNARE COMBINATIONS	52
16TH NOTE RHYTHMS WITH SNARE TOM COMBINATIONS	53
16TH NOTE ACCENTS ON TOMS	54
16TH NOTE RHYTHMS WITH TOM ROLLS AND RESTS	55
SOLO EXERCISE	56
STUDENT PRACTICAL SUMMARY	57

CHAPTER 4 — 58

DOTTED NOTES AND 16TH NOTE VARIATIONS	59
DOTTED NOTE AND SYNCOPATION PART #2	60
16TH NOTE VARATIONS EXPLAINED	61
16TH NOTE VARIATION #1	62
16TH NOTE VARIATION #2	63
16TH NOTE VARIATION #3	64
16TH NOTE VARIATION #4	65
16TH NOTE VARIATION #5	66
16TH NOTE VARIATION #6	67
16TH NOTE VARIATION #7	68
QUARTER NOTE WITH MIXED 16TH NOTE VARIATION	69
8TH NOTE WITH MIXED 16TH NOTE VARIATION	70
16TH NOTES WITH 16TH VARIATIONS	71
ALL 16TH NOTES VARIATIONS ON SNARE	72
MIXED RHYTHMS WITH VARIATIONS ON SNARE	73
MIXED RHYTHMS WITH VARIATIONS ON TOMS	74
QUARTER 8THS 16TH NOTE VARIATIONS COMBINATION STUDY	75
QUARTER 8THS 16TH NOTE VARIATIONS WITH RESTS	76
16TH NOTE RHYTHMS WITH VARIATIONS	77
16TH NOTE RHYTHMS WITH MIXED VARIATIONS	78
16TH NOTE VARIATIONS WITH SNARE ROLLS	79
16TH NOTE VARIATIONS WITH TOM ROLLS	80
8TH & 16TH SEPERATION EXCERISES	81
8TH & 16TH NOTE RHYTHM TRANSITIONS	82
MIXED NOTES AND VARAIATION RHYTHMS PATTERNS	83
8THS OVER 16TH RYHTHM PATTERNS	84
MIXED NOTE SNARE DISPLACEMENTS	85
8TH OVER 16TH RHYTHM AND SNARE DISPLACEMENTS	86
MIXED HIGH HAT RHYTHMS #1	87
MIXED HIGH HAT RHYTHMS #2	88
SOLO EXERCISE	89
STUDENT PRACTICAL SUMMARY	90
TIME SIGNATURES AND COUNTING	91
ODD TIME SIGNATURES	92
COMPOUND TIME SIGNATURES	93

CHAPTER 5 — 94

TRIPLETS EXPLAINED	95
QUARTER NOTE WITH TRIPLETS	96
8TH NOTES WITH TRIPLETS	97
16TH NOTES WITH TRIPLETS	98
QUARTER 8THS 16THS NOTES WITH TRIPLETS	99
8TH NOTE TRIPLET ACCENTS	100

8TH NOTE TRIPLET REST	101
MIXED NOTE AND REST EXERCISE	102
8TH NOTE TRIPLET RHYTHMS	103
8TH NOTE TRIPLET RHYTHMS WITH ROLLS	104
8TH NOTE MATHEMATICAL RHYTHMS WITH IRREGULAR TRIPLETS	105
8TH NOTE VARIATION RHYTHMS WITH WITH IRREGULAR TRIPLETS	106
SOLO EXERCISE	107
STUDENT PRACTICAL SUMMARY	108

CHAPTER 6 — 109

16TH NOTE TRIPLET EXPLAINED	110
QUARTER NOTE WITH 16TH NOTE TRIPLETS	111
8TH NOTE WITH 16TH NOTE TRIPLETS	112
16TH NOTE WITH 16TH NOTE TRIPLETS	113
8TH NOTE TRIPLETS WITH 16TH NOTE TRIPLETS	114
TRIPLET MIXED COMBINATION PART #1	115
TRIPLET MIXED COMBINATIONS PART #2	116
16TH NOTE TRIPLET RESTS	117
IRREGULAR TRIPLET REST EXERCISE	118
MIXED NOTES WITH REST	119
VARIATIIONS WITH IRREGULAR TRIPLETS	120
8TH NOTE TRIPLET RHYTHMS WITH IRREGULAR ROLLS ON SNARE	121
8TH NOTE TRIPLETS WITH IRREGULAR ROLLS ON TOMS	122
8TH NOTE TRIPLET RHYTHMS WITH IRREGULAR RESTS	123
8TH NOTE TRIPLETS WITH IRREGULAR RESTED TOM ROLLS	124
STUDENT PRACTICAL SUMMARY	125

CHAPTER 7 — 126

32ND NOTES EXPLAINED	127
QUARTER WITH 32ND NOTES	128
8TH NOTES WITH 32ND NOTES	129
BROKEN 32ND NOTES	130
16TH NOTES WITH 32ND NOTES	131
RESTED 32ND NOTES ON SNARE	132
QUARTER NOTE RHYTHMS WITH 32ND NOTE ROLLS	133
8TH NOTE RHYTHMS WITH 32ND NOTE ROLLS	134
8TH NOTE TRIPLET RHYTHMS WITH 32ND NOTE ROLLS	135
16TH NOTE RHYTHMS WITH 32ND NOTE ROLLS	136
MIXED RHYTHMS WITH RESTED 32 NOTES ON SNARE	137
MIXED RHYTHMS WITH RESTED 32ND NOTE ROLLS ON TOMS	138
MIXED RHYTHMS WITH ALL NOTE COMBINATIONS ROLLS	139
MIXED RHYTHMS WITH ALL NOTE COMBINATONS ROLLS ON TOMS	140
ULTIMATE MIXED NOTE COMBINATIONS PART #1	141
ULTIMATE MIXED NOTE COMBINATIONS WITH RESTS PART #2	142
ULTIMATE MIXED NOTE COMBINATIONS WITH VARIATIONS	143

INTRODUCTION

Hi, I'm Joel Hammond, and I'm thrilled to welcome you to The Drum Hub—your all-in-one guide to learning drums, from beginner to advanced levels.

Drumming has been my passion for over 25 years, taking me from my early days in the UK to building my own music school here in Australia. Throughout my journey of performing, touring, and teaching, I've worked with students of all ages—ranging from six to sixty—and developed a deep understanding of how different people learn. That's why I've designed this book to be fun, engaging, and easy to follow, no matter where you are on your drumming journey.

This book is more than just exercises and theory. It's a complete, step-by-step guide that will help you build a solid foundation in technique, develop a strong understanding of music notation, and most importantly, enjoy the process. Whether you're picking up sticks for the first time or refining your skills, you'll find lessons that challenge and inspire you, all while keeping drumming exciting and creative.

Drumming is more than just beats and rhythms—it's a form of self-expression, a source of energy, and a way to connect with music on a deeper level. So grab your sticks, get comfortable, and let's dive into the world of drumming together. By the time you reach the last page, you won't just be a better drummer—you'll have the confidence, knowledge, and passion to take your drumming anywhere you want to go.

Let's get started!

DRUM KIT APPENDIX

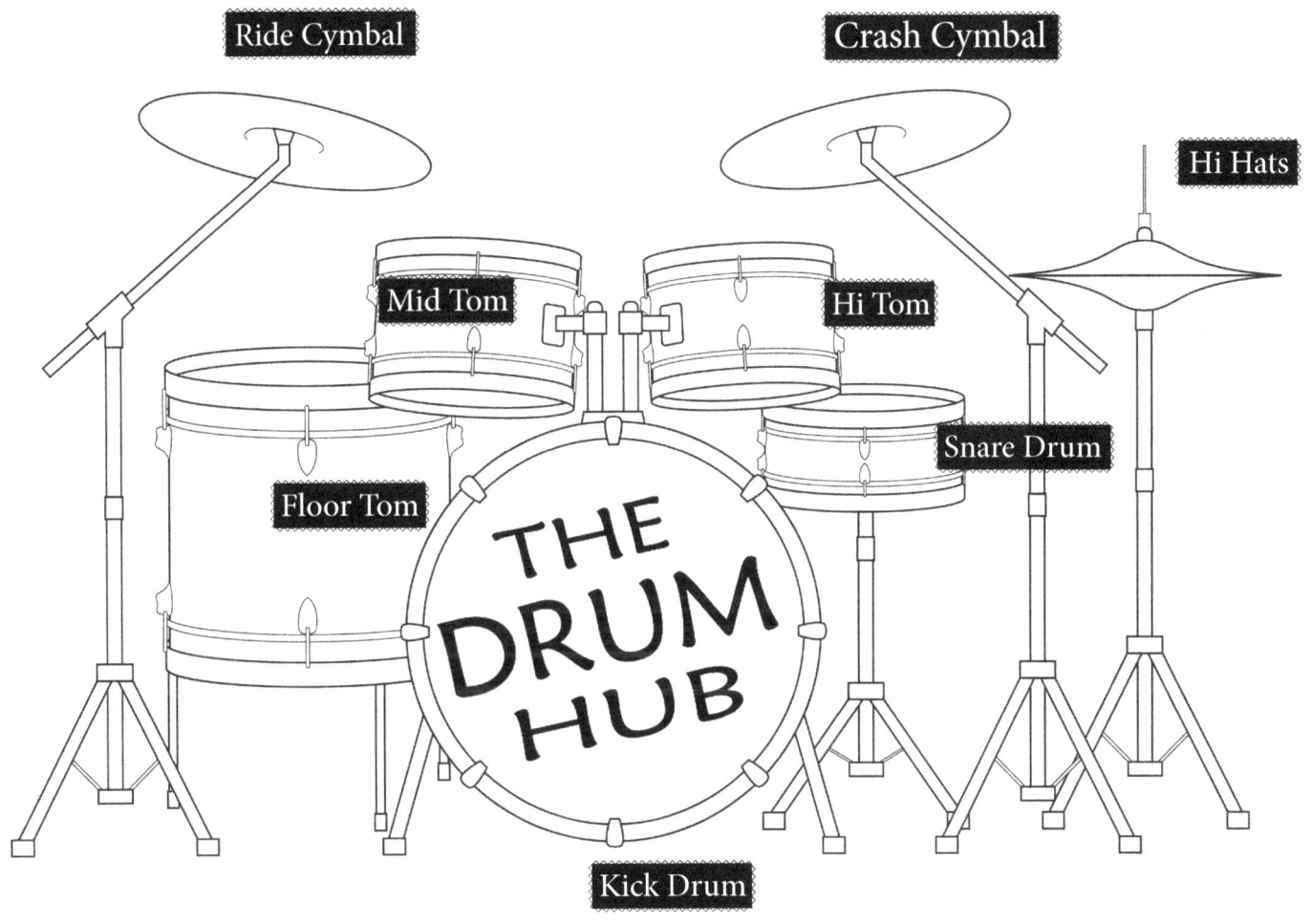

CORRECT STICK PLACEMENT AND POSTURE

Correctly grab your sticks with your index fingers and thumbs

Carefully wrap fingers around base of drum stick

Straight posture with sticks at 15-degree angle

Position yourself with a nice V-shape with relaxed grip

Chapter 1

NOTE SCALE

In this book we will learn how to count our whole notes right through to our 32nd notes.
Each note has its own distinctive count, please take note that we are still only counting to 4.

STAFF LINES AND MEANINGS

A staff line is a measure of 5 horizontal lines bounded by two verticial lines which will contain a time signiture and a musical cleff of some sort. Each line represents a different part of the drums.
The snare is a very common part of the drums vocabulary, hence it has a lot more abbreviations

DYNAMIC TERMS AND MEANINGS

Music dynamics refer to the variation in loudness or intensity of a music piece. Dynamics add expression and emotion to music, shapng the overall musical experience. Here are some key terms and their meanings.

1. Pianissimo **(pp)** Play very softly.

2. Piano **(p)** Play softly.

3. Mezza Piano **(mp)** Play moderately softly.

4. Mezza Forte **(mf)** Play moderately loud.

5. Forte **(f)** Play loud.

6. Fortissimo **(ff)** Play very loud.

7. Fortississimo **(fff)** Play extremely loud.

8. Cresendo Gradually get louder.

9. Decresendo Gradually get softer.

10. Sforzando **(sfz or fz)** A strong sudden accent.

11. Diminuedo **(dim)** Gradually getting softer, similar to decresendo.

Although there are many types of **Tempo marks** here are just a few common **Tempo dynamics** are as followed.

SLOW
       1. Larghissimo **(15-20 Bpm)**
       2. Lento **(40 - 50 Bpm)**
       3. Adagio **(60-70 Bpm)**

MEDIUM
       1. Andente **(72-80 Bpm)**
       2. Moderato **(85-95 Bpm)**
       3. Allegretto **(100-115 Bpm)**

FAST
       1. Allegro **(115- 130 Bpm)**
       2. Vivacissimo **(140-150 Bpm)**
       3. Presto **(160-175 Bpm)**

WHOLE NOTE, HALF NOTE AND QUARTER NOTE AND REST EXPLANATION

First of all we have to understand a 4/4 Time Signature. The top 4 = the amount of beats in the bar, while the bottom 4 = the type or value of note.
With the whole note beat, a whole note = 4/4 or 4 qtr notes in the bar.
The half note = 2 qtr notes per beat

THE DRUM HUB

REPEATS SIGN AND 1ST AND 2ND ENDINGS EXPLAINED

Ok guys we have some important information here regarding the repeat sign and first and second endings. In music we want to keep our staff lines as clean and practical as possible, less clutter the better. Repeat signs are essential for navigating through musical compositions efficiently, allowing performers to play sections multiple times without having to write out or read redundant music.

Whilst 1st and 2nd endings provide a way to repeat sections while incorporating variations in the musical content, it will help you streamline notation by avoiding unnecessary repetition of the same material.

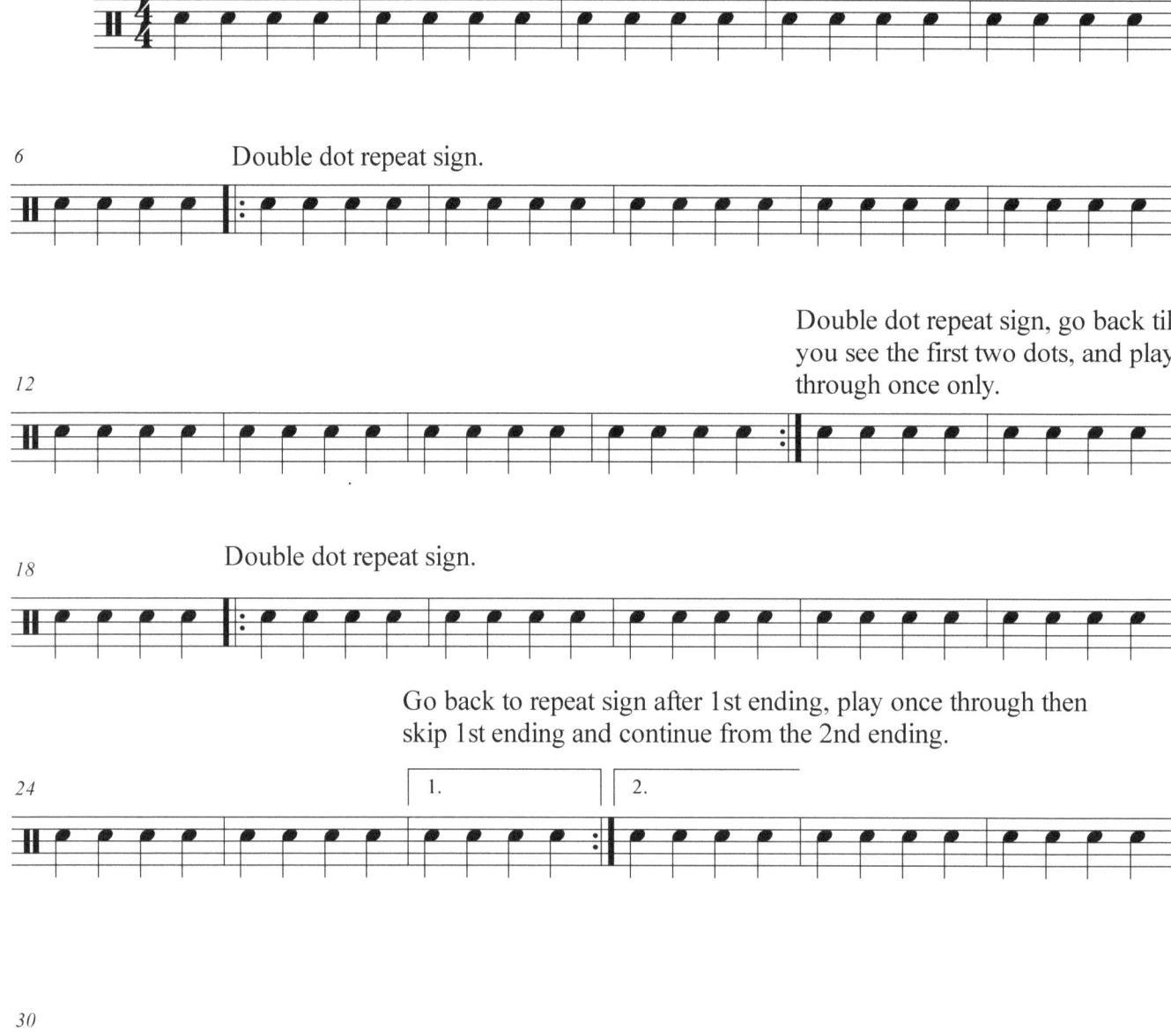

Double bar line indicates end of music.

UNDERSTANDING DA CAPO, DEL SEGNO, AND D.S. AL FINE AND CODA

Ok guys Just like the previous page understanding " D.C. al Fine and the D.C. al Coda in music notation involves navigating the structures of a piece of music.
These notations help composers and arrangers structure music more efficiently and provide variations in repeated sections. Go slow guys and read the sections below carefully, good luck.

WHOLE NOTE HALF NOTES REST

Welcome to chapter 1, learning the whole note and half note with their rests.
Remember to go slow and get your count correct. We can always go faster as we get better.

Remember the whole note only gets 1 hit per bar and lasts the duration of the count to 4.

The half note will get 2 hits per bar on the 1 and 3 count only.

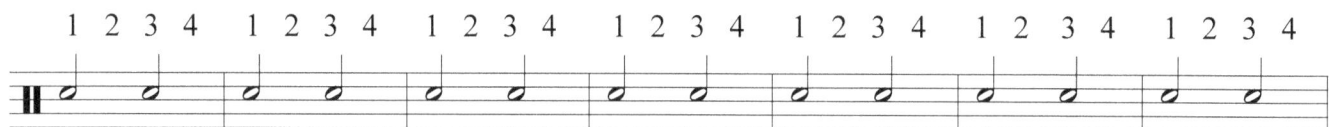

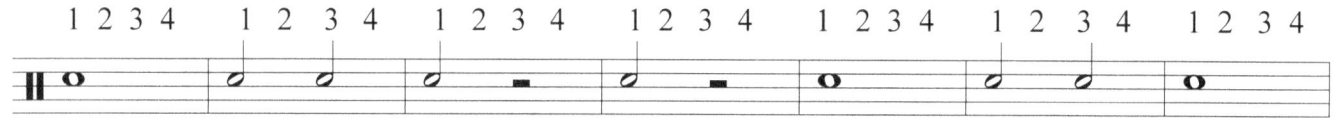

Ok now try to play the remaining bars without the help of the numbers, be sure to count out loud.

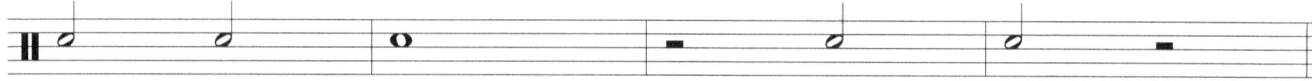

QUARTER NOTE AND QTR NOTE REST

Remember our 4/4 time signature.
There are 4 beats to the bar, the top 4 is how many beats in the bar, and the bottom 4 is the type or value of the note.
The qtr note will get 4 hits to the bar on all 4 counts e.g. (1 2 3 4)

These are what our quarter note rests look like, remember a rest will get a count in value but will not get a hit. We must stil count the number but skip playing the beat

Now try playing the remaining qtr notes and qtr rests without the numbers to help you.

Well done! You have now finished your introduction of the quarter note and rest.
I hope you enjoyed this exercise.
Remember it's very important to count out loud as you are playing.

THE DRUM HUB

QUARTER NOTE FOOT AND REST EXERCISE

In this exercise we are adding two parts of the drums, we are now using the kick drum and snare drum stafflines. So now we have two bits of information on our staff lines. Remember to count slow and try alternating your sticking by doing left right left right hand motions.

60-90 bpm

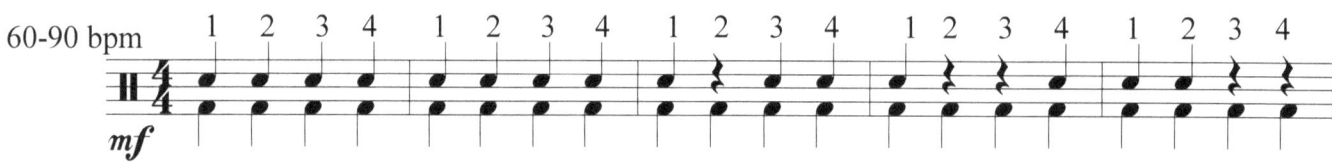

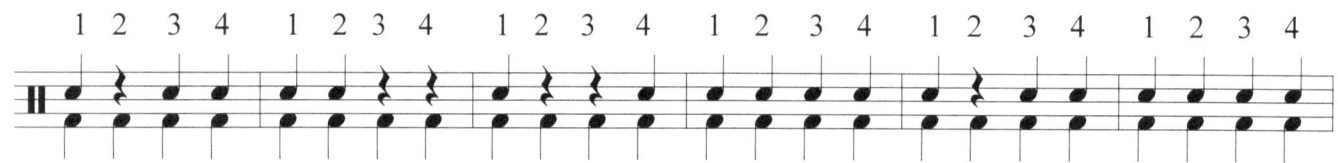

Notice how we are kicking on all 4 counts, we are using our kick drum as a 4/4 metronome, you want to keep a nice steady pace to begin with.

Now try the last remaining bars without the numbers, so you can get used to the qtr note count.

WHOLE HALF QUARTER MIXED NOTE STUDY

So hopefully by now we should be able to play our note study without the numbers to help us.
Remember to always count out loud and use your alternating sticking.

60-90 bpm

Alternate sticking.

THE DRUM HUB

MIXED NOTE AND REST COMBINATION STUDY, PART#1

Skill tester time, there are plenty of mixed notes and rest in this combination study.
Remember to go slow, count your notes, and remember the length of time our rests equal in our count.

QUARTER NOTE RHYTHMS 4/4 ROCK BEAT

Welcome to the 4/4 rock rhythm, on this page we will learn how to play a simple beat, now we will be using 3 parts of our body to play, plus 3 parts of the drum kit. Our high hat, snare and kick drum. I have broken it down into 2 parts (A) and Part (B)

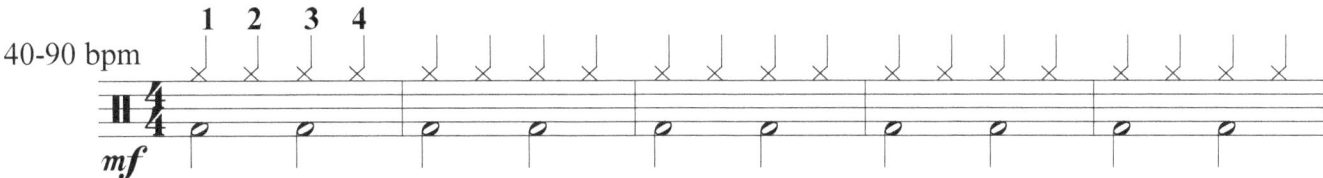

In this part (A) section notice we are hitting the top staff line which repersents the High Hat which will get a count of 1 2 3 4. And on the bottom line which represents the kick drum on the 1 and 3 count, Slowly play these together simultaneously. Remember to always keep count on the High Hat.

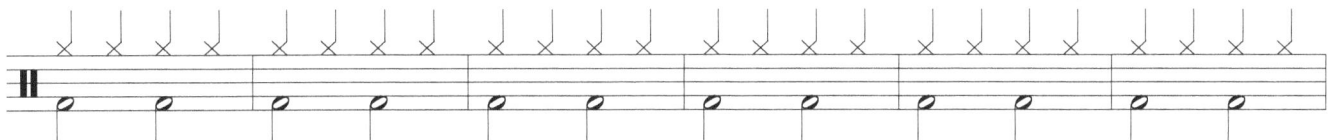

In this section part (B) notice we are only focussing on the high hat and snare line now. We still want to hit the high hat on the count of 1 2 3 4, while the snare drum will be played on the 2 and 4

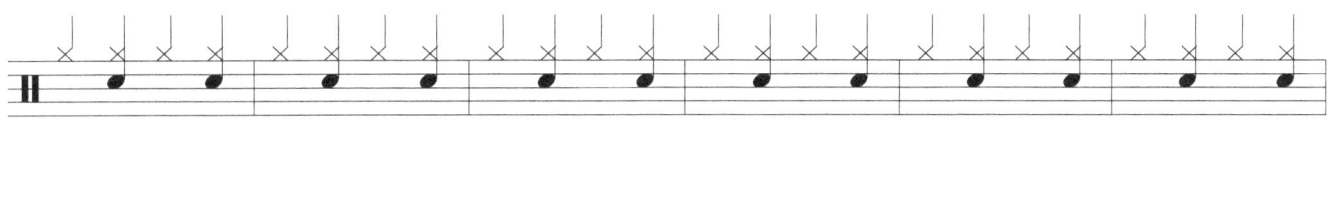

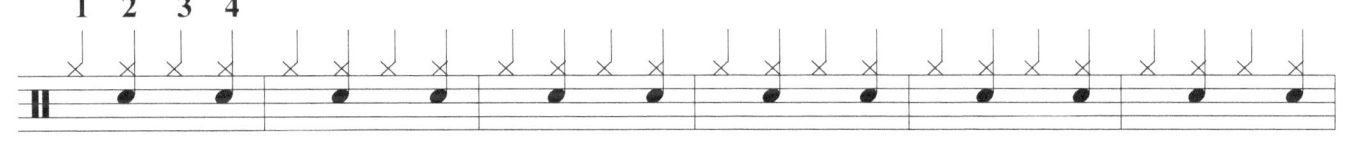

Well done! Now it's time to combine both part (A) and (B) together to create the 4/4 rock beat. Remember to keep count on the High Hat, 1 2 3 4. The kick is on 1 and 3 and the snare is the opposite on the 2 and 4. Start super slow and you will gradually get faster.

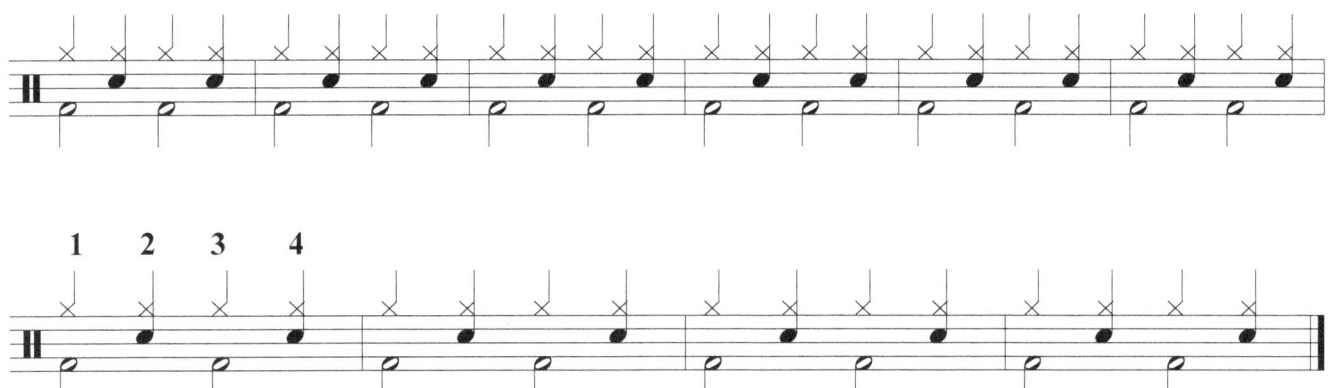

THE DRUM HUB

QUARTER NOTE RHYTHM WITH ROLLS AND REST

Now we should be more competent with the 4/4 rhythm, now it's time to play our rhythm section with rolls and rests on the snare. Make sure you count your qtr note rhyhtm, 1 2 3 4, and count your rolls out on the snare drum. Have fun!

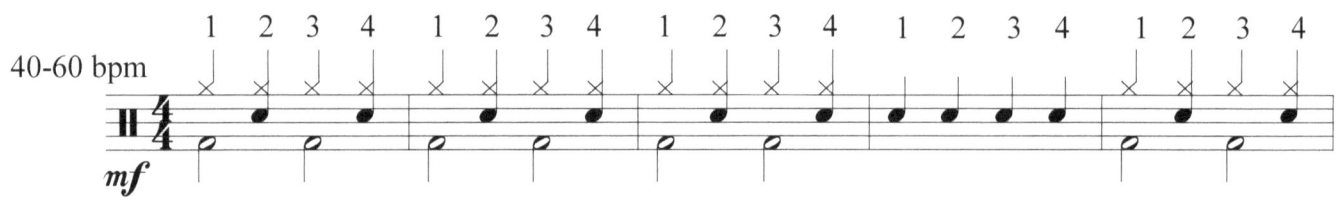

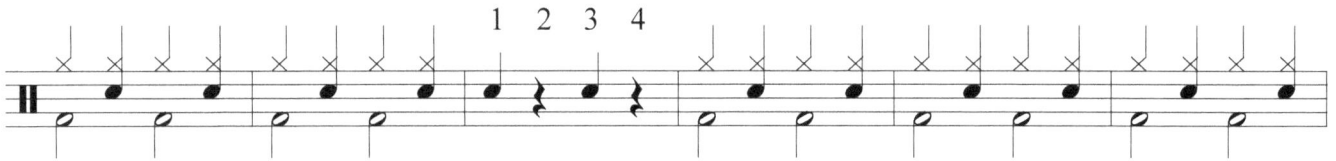

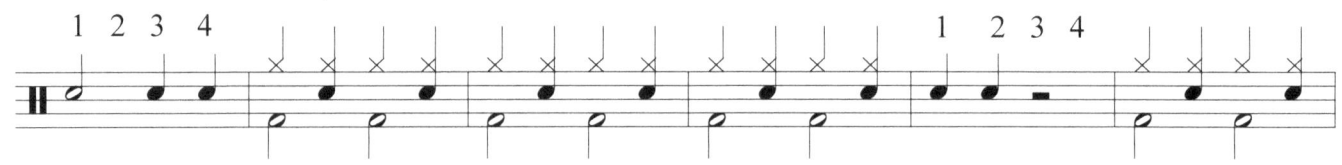

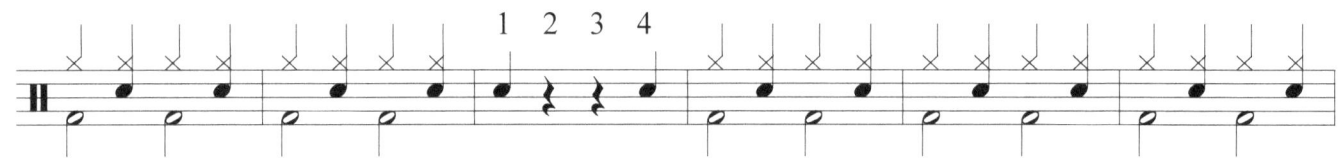

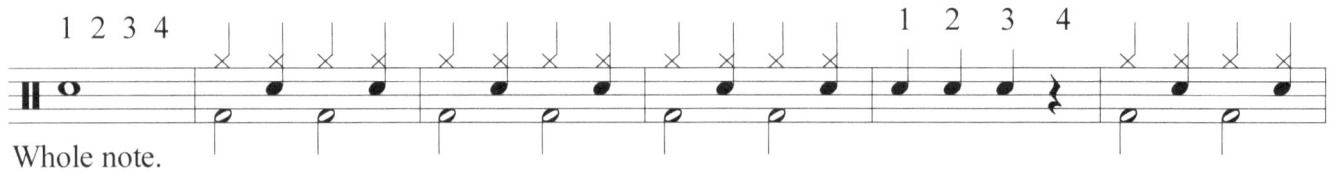

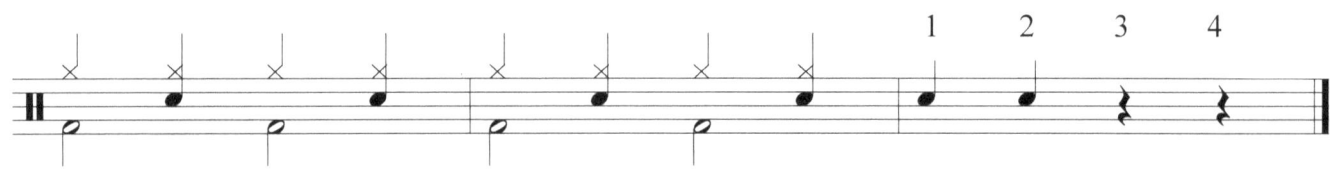

MIXED QUARTER NOTE TOM ROLLS

Time to step it up, now we are going to introduce our qtr note tom rolls around the kit. Now remember each staff line represents a different drum. Be sure to analyze your **staff line index in the front of the book,** and get familar with them. Take it slow and be sure to count out loud.

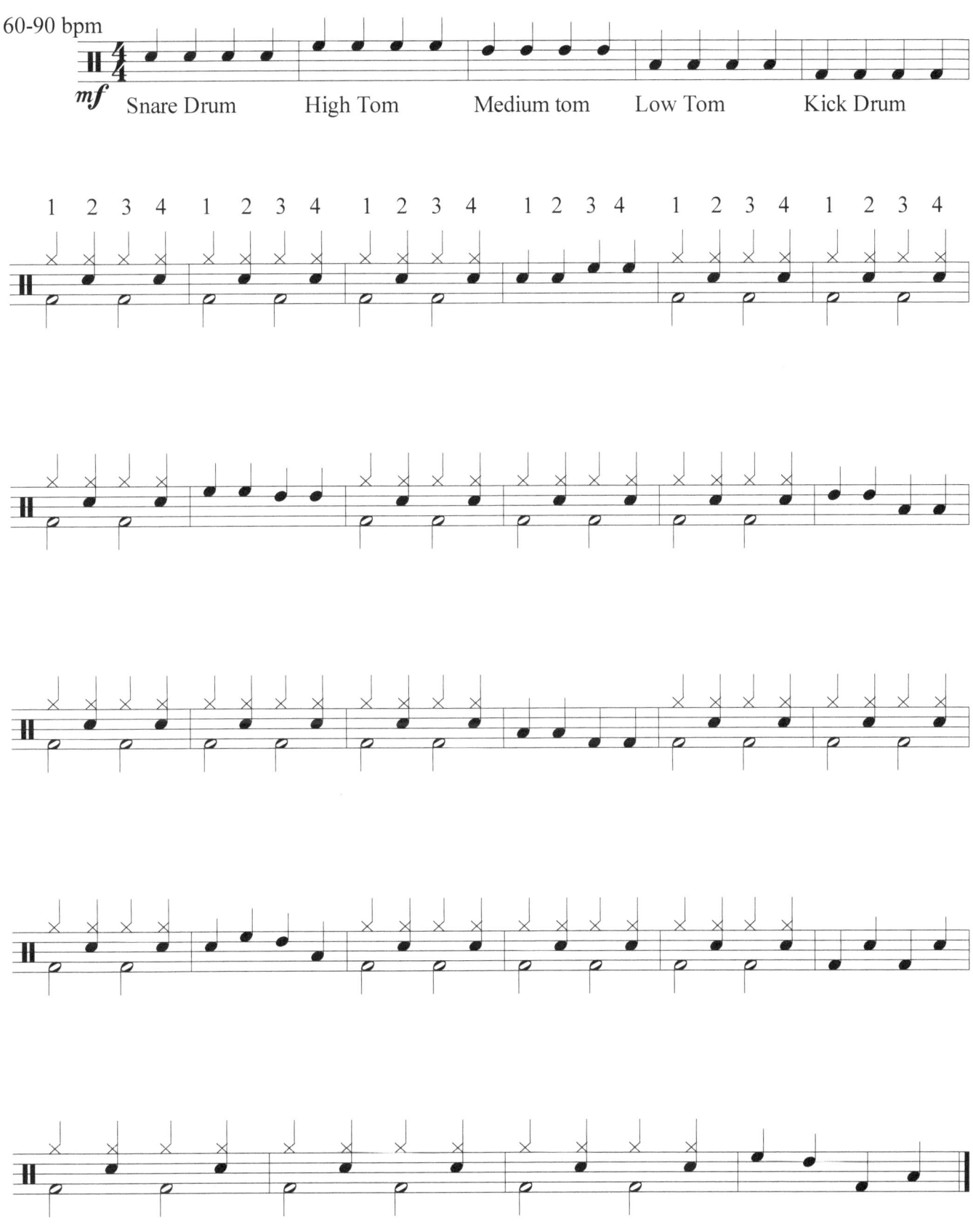

SKILL TESTER #1

Now it's time to try this Skill Tester. It's a summary of what we have been learning in chapter #1.
Remember to go slowly, count out loud. Have fun!

60-90 Bpm

Now as you can see we are adding in a crash cymbal on the number 1 count after our roll. Please refer to your **staff lines and meanings** in the beginning of this book.
All we want to do is move the number 1 count off the high hat up onto the crash cymbal with your kick.

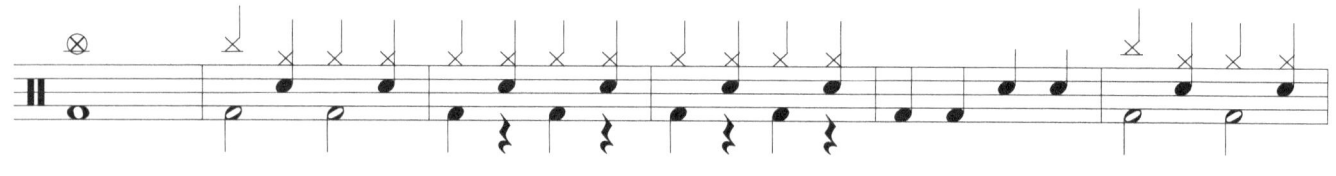

SOLO EXERCISE PART #1

Welcome guys to your first solo section. We have double dot repeat signs, 1st and 2nd endings and our D.S. al Fine repeats as well. If you have trouble understanding these, please go back to the front of the book and reacquaint yourself with the terms and meanings.

STUDENT PRACTICAL SUMMARY

On these blank staff lines use your bars to practise writing down the notation that you have learnt thus far. Try adding in your rests and write out some of you're favourite rhythms. Have fun!

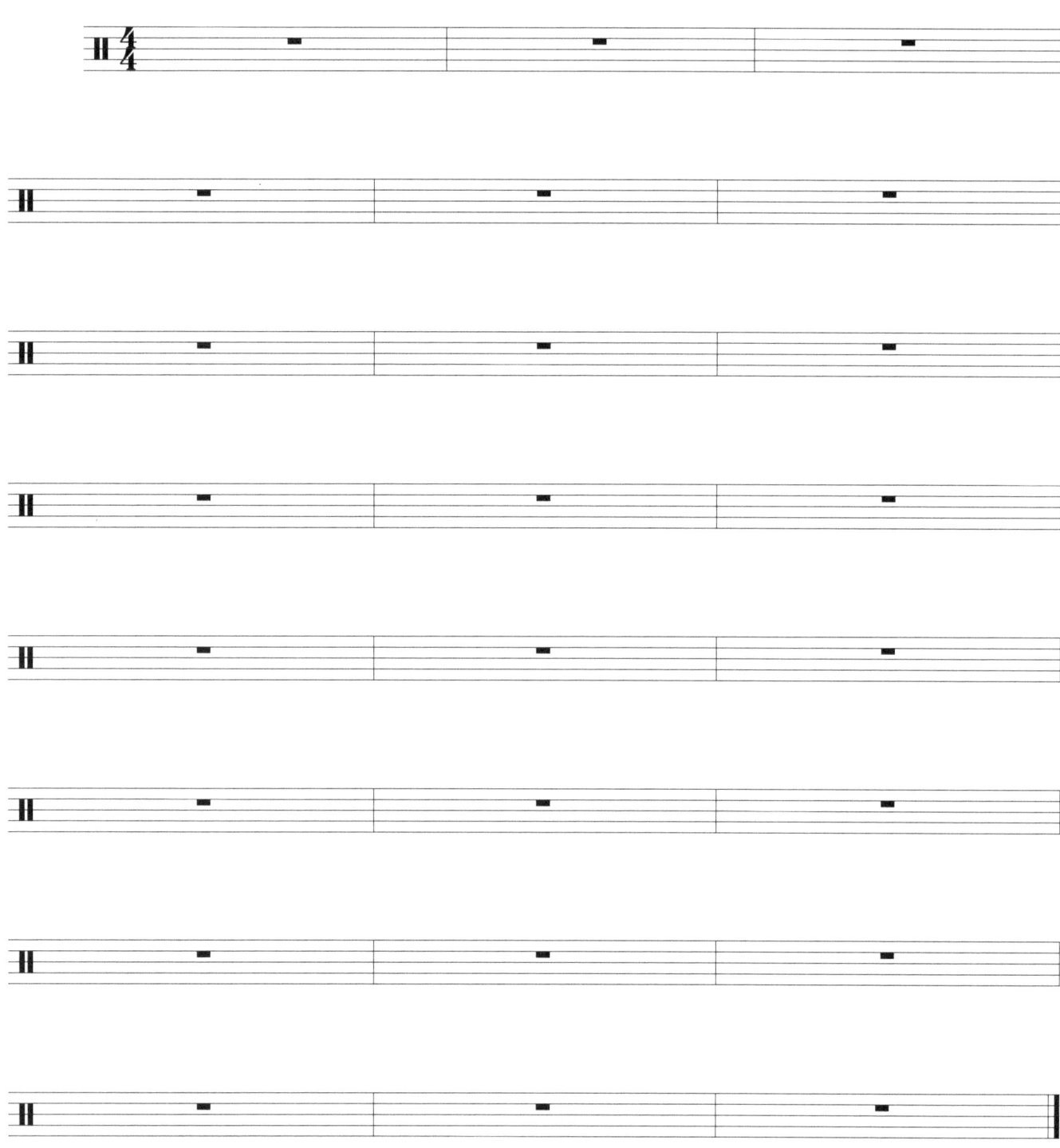

Chapter 2

UNDERSTANDING THE 8TH NOTE

Congratulations! Welcome to chapter 2, on this page we are going to understand how to divide a qtr note into two 8th notes. With the qtr note, imagine cutting the qtr note into two halves, each half repersenting an 8th note. **(See notes below)**

Qtr Notes counted as 1 2 3 4   1 2 3 4   1 2 3 4   1 2 3 4   1 2 3 4

Now as you can see we have doubled each qtr note into to 8th notes, The whole cut and double approach splitting the qtr note in two. We now have a brand new count.!

8th note is counted as   1 + 2 + 3 + 4 +   1 + 2 + 3 + 4 +   1 + 2 + 3 + 4 +   1 + 2 + 3 + 4 +

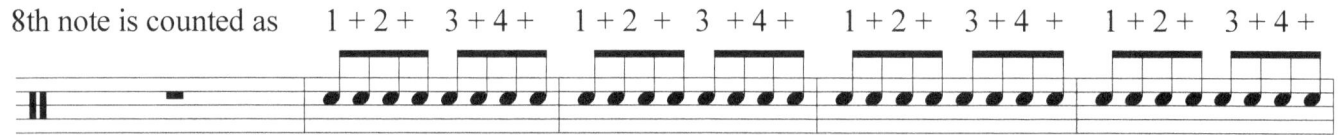

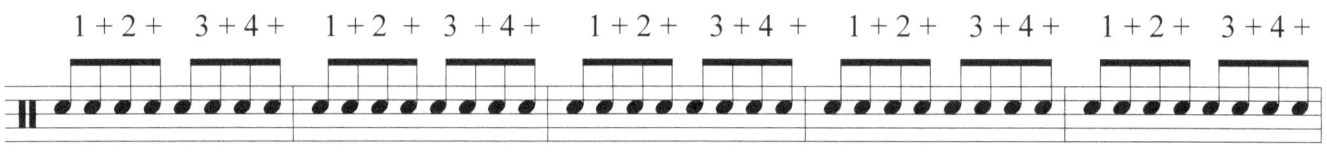

Notice our qtr note is still hiden inside the new 8th note count.

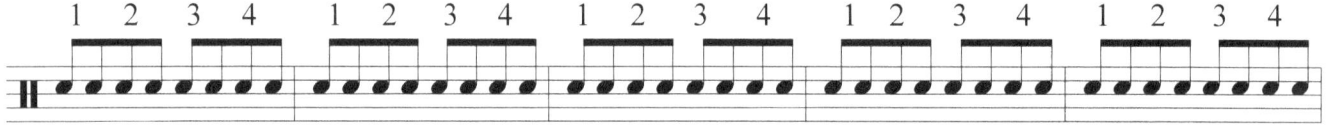

Our primary qtr note is still there but see how we have doubled the count to 1+2+3+4+

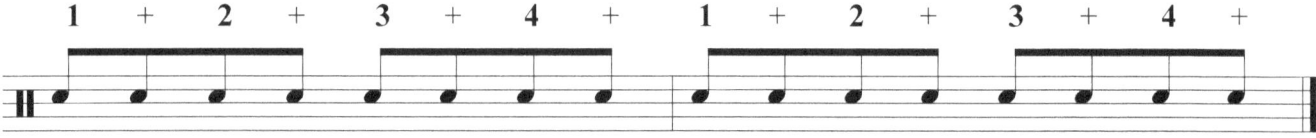

QUARTERS AND 8TH SNARE EXERCISES

Now it's time to try our mixed note combinatios on the snare, remember to count qtrs at 1 2 3 4 and our new 8th notes at 1+2+3+4+
Go slow and count out loud.

60-90 bpm

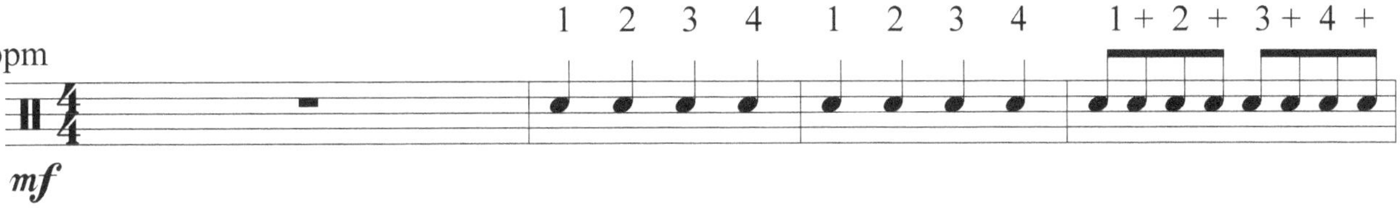

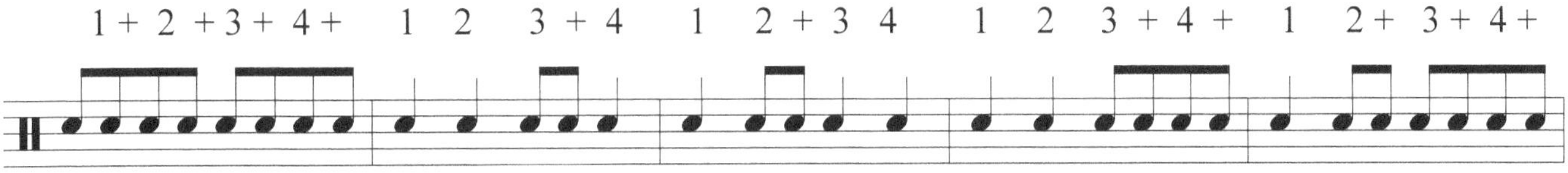

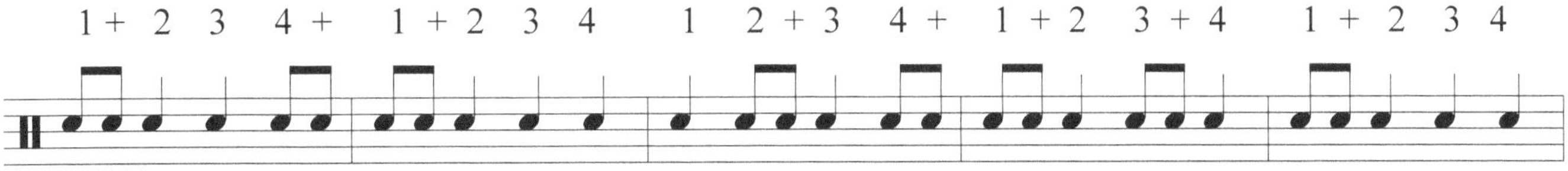

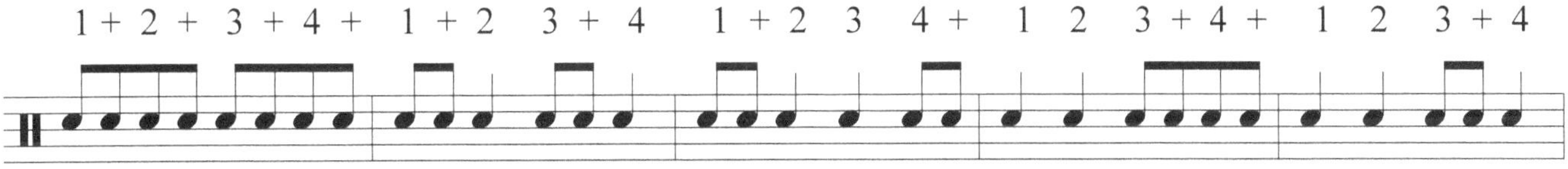

Hope you are starting to get comfortable with counting your qtrs and 8th note combinations.
Now try counting your bars without the help of the numbers. Good luck!

THE DRUM HUB

QUARTERS AND 8TH WITH FOOT EXERCISES

In this qtr and 8th note snare exercise, we want to add our foot on the bottom staff line to add that qtr note metronome feel to help us keep in time. This will allow us to get those 8th notes in on the snare, they will be played in between each kick on the bottom line. Remember to count out loud.

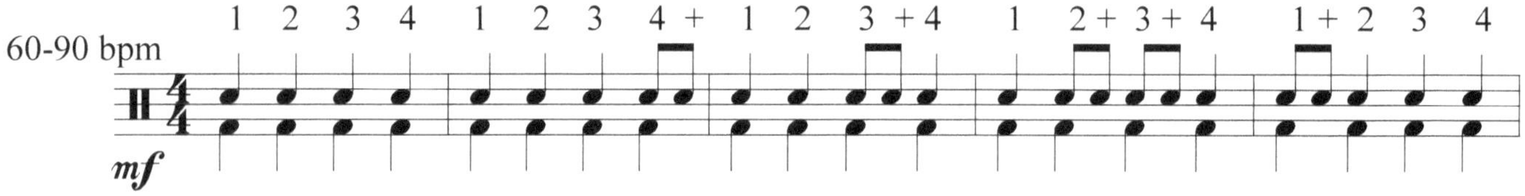

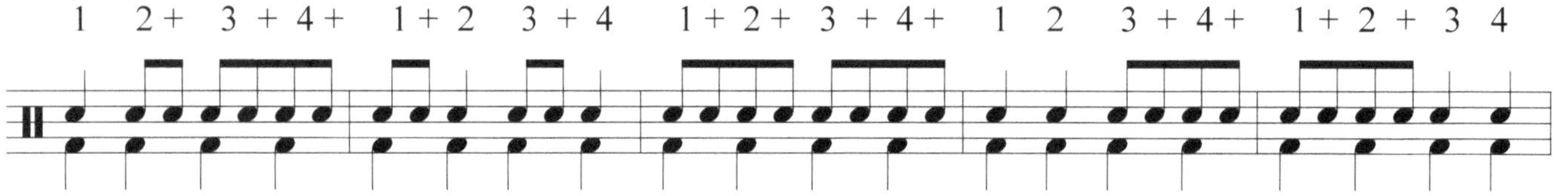

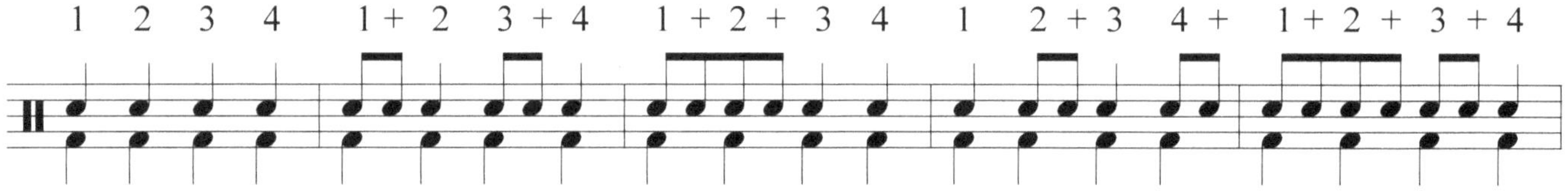

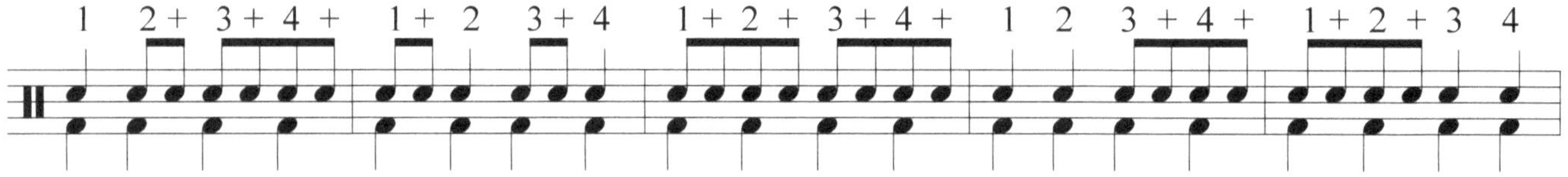

Ok now try without the number to help you, but remember to keep that kick drum nice and steady to help keep an even tempo thoughout.

UNDERSTAND THE 8TH NOTE REST

Just like in Chapter #1 learning the whole, half and qtr note rest, we are now moving onto the 8th note rest. Throughout this book we will learn all notes and their accompanied rests.
Remember with the rests we count their value in time but skip playing the beat.

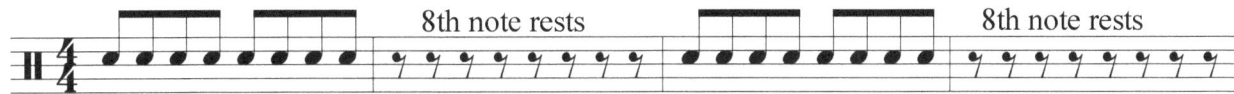

As you can see here I have rested the + of 1, you will still count the whole bar as 1+2+3+4+
but you will count the 8th note rest as a beat but will not play the rest as it is silent.

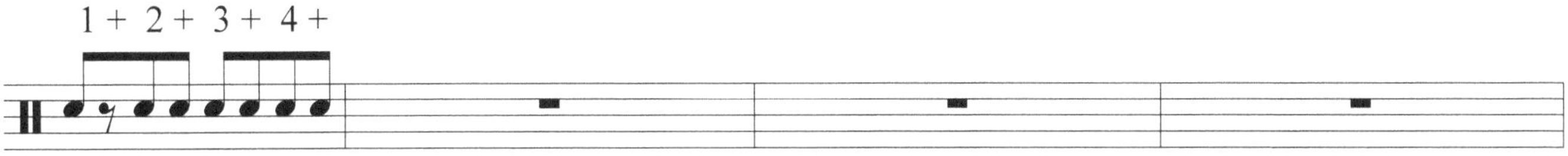

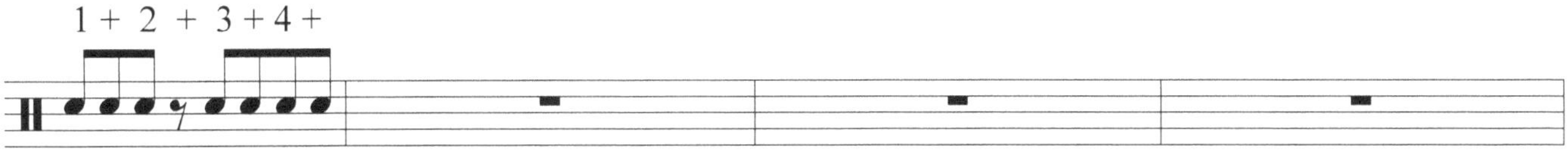

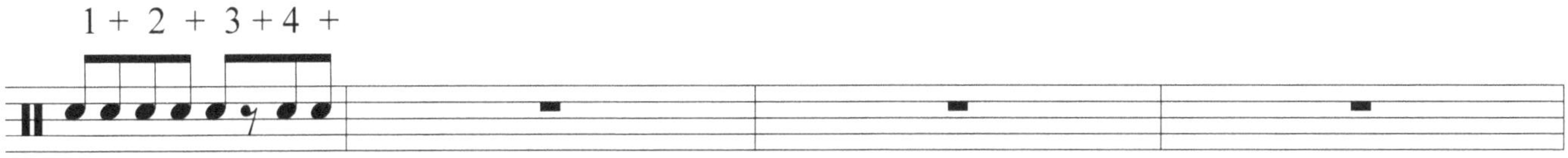

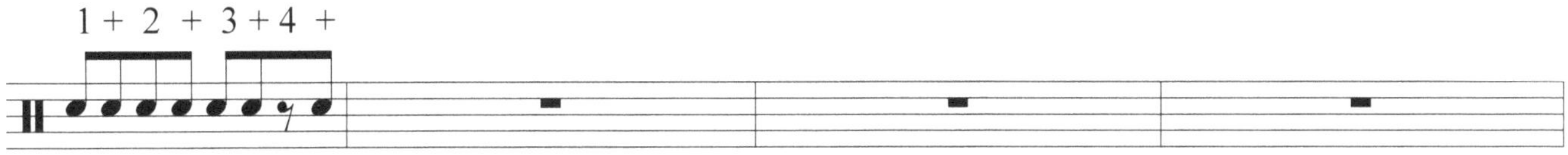

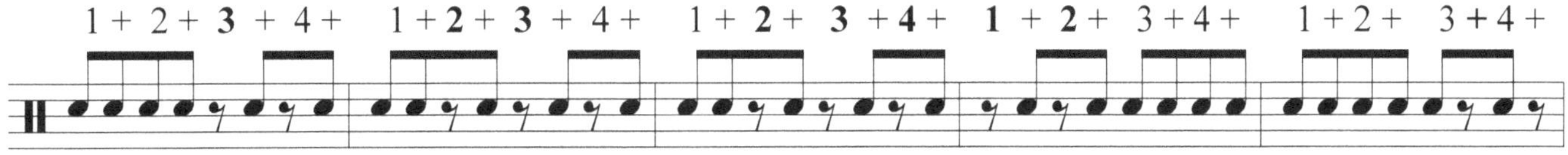

Well done, I hope this helped you understand the 8th note rest.
Remember the A. B. C's of drumming. (ALWAYS BE COUNTING)

THE DRUM HUB

QUARTER AND 8TH SNARE EXERCISE WITH RESTS

On this page we are going to have our mixed qtr notes and 8th notes with their accompanied rests.
There will be a lot of information on the staff lines, so remember to count your notes and rests and their values.
Start slow and count out loud. Good luck and have fun.

60-90 bpm

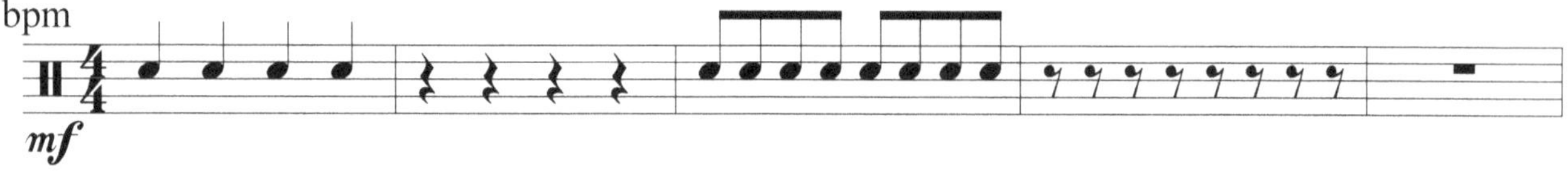

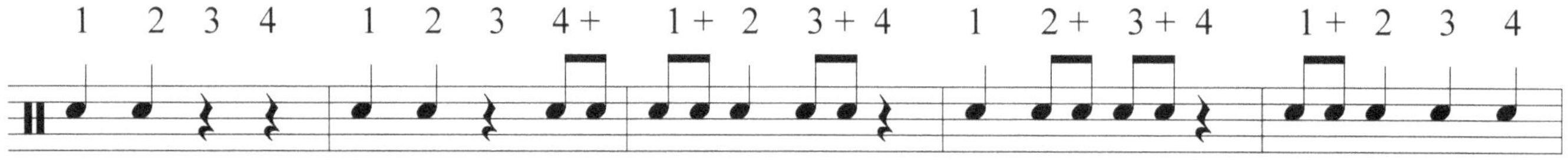

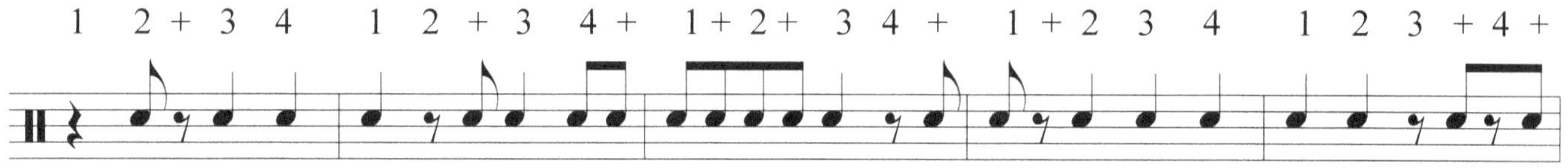

Now try the remaining bars without the numbers, be sure to count the values of your rests, remember they have a numeric value that equals the distance from each primary number. Go slow and count carefully.

26   THE DRUM HUB

QUARTER AND 8TH NOTE REST WITH FOOT

Just like the previous page we have a lot of rests in this exercise, we are now adding a foot on the kick drum to keep that nice steady tempo. Be sure to go slow and allow those rests to be spaced out equally.

Once agian, now try without the help of the numbers, go slowly and study your rests.

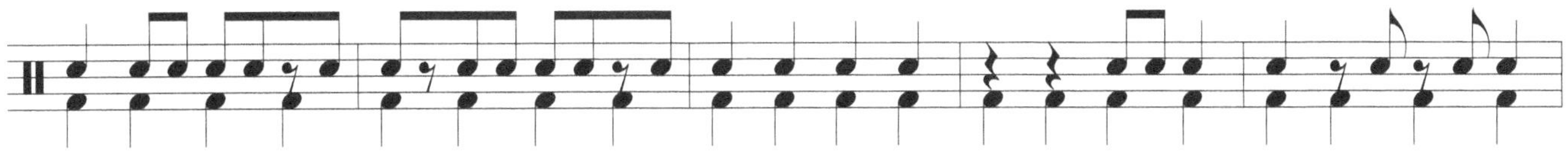

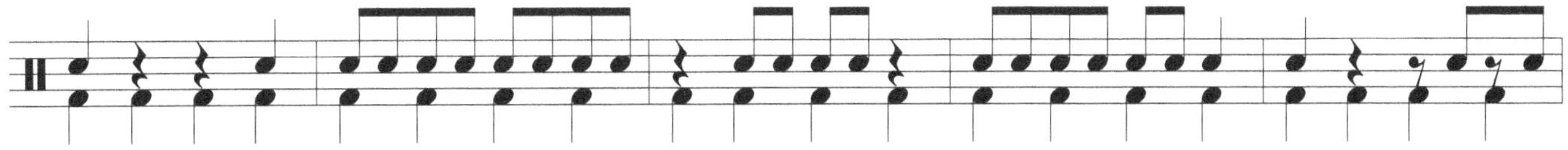

HIGH HAT AND FOOT SEPARATION EXCERCISES

On this page we want to develop our hand and foot independence, this is going to help us learn harder rhythm beats thoughout this book. Notice there is no snare, we want to focus directly on our hand and foot separation exercises.

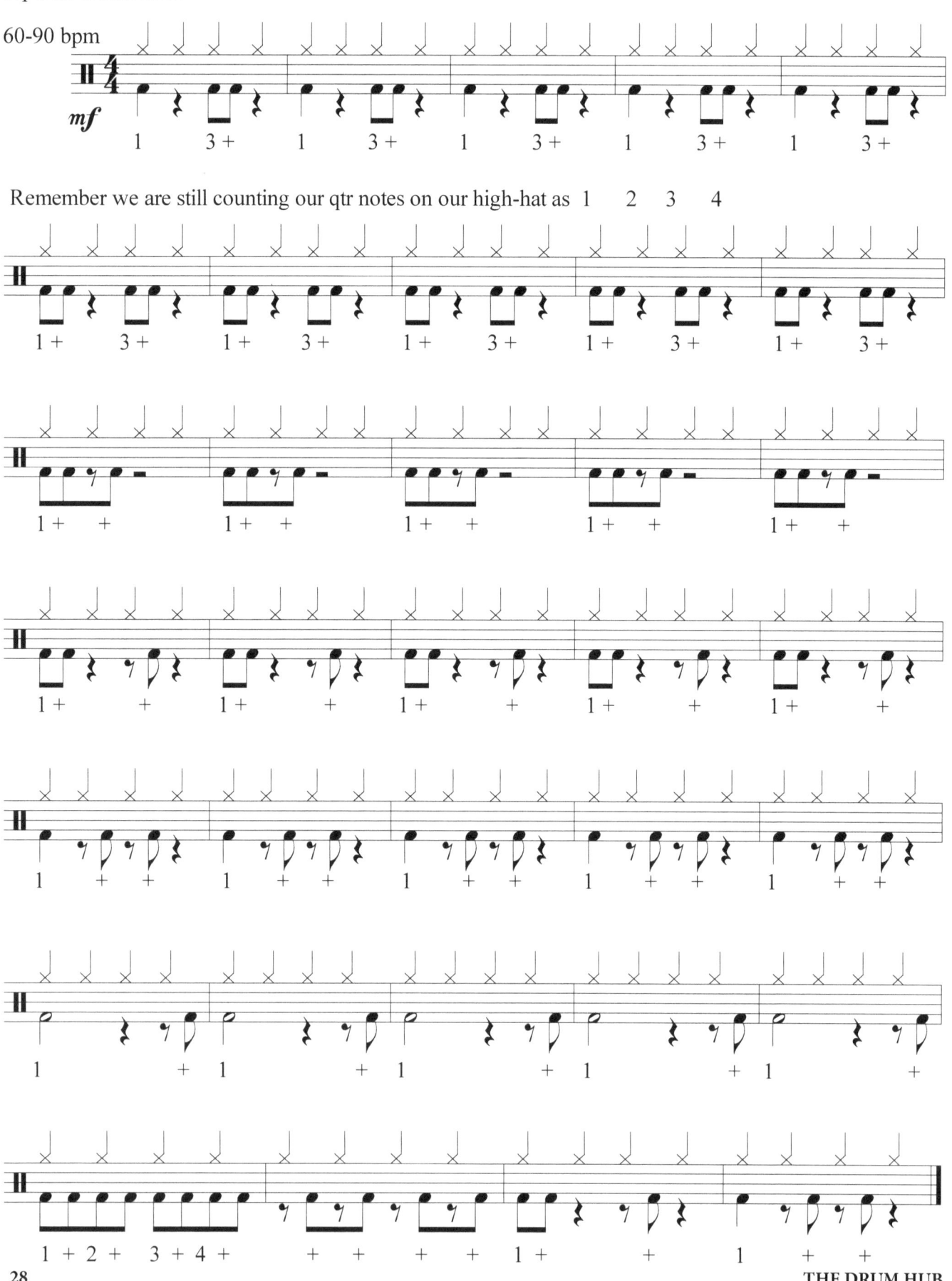

THE DRUM HUB

QUARTER AND 8TH NOTE REST WITH FOOT

Now like the previous page, we are now adding the snare in, be mindful that we are still using our seperation movements, as the hand comes up the foot in goes down. Be sure to start slow and use your A.B.C's method.

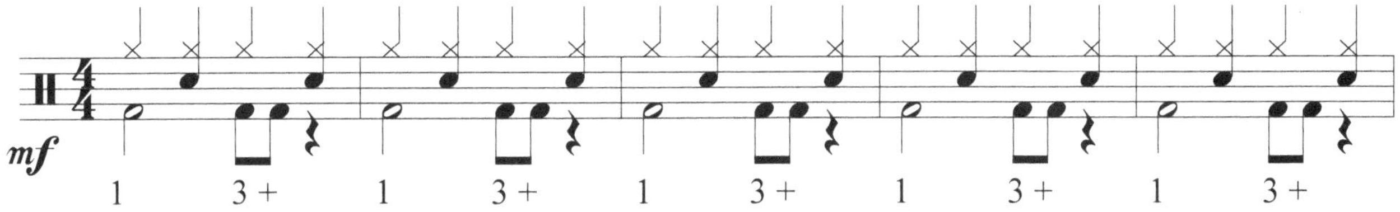

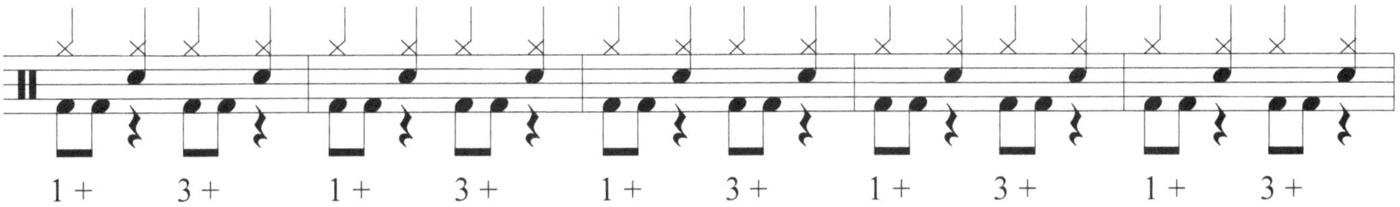

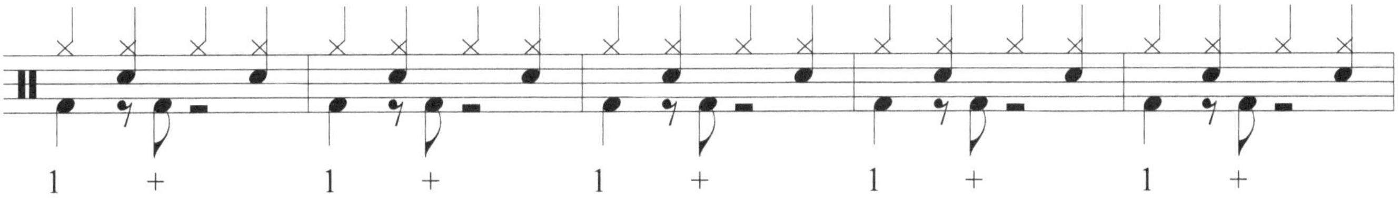

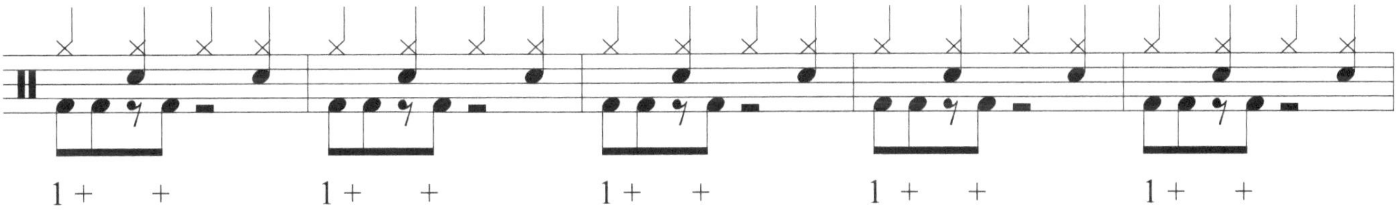

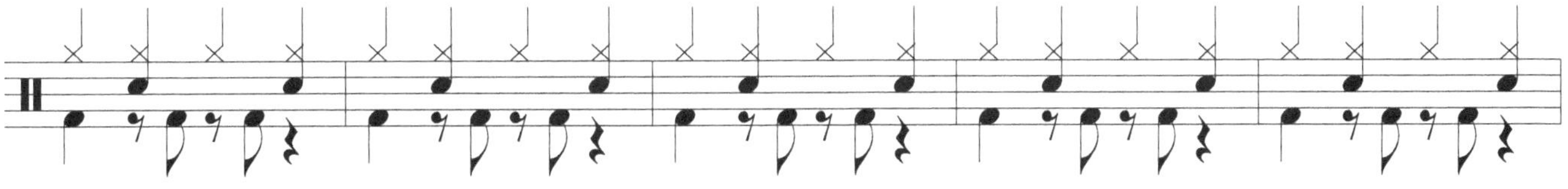

As you can see, I have changed our high-hat line to our ride cymbal, notice our staves are no longer the top line. You will play with an open hand type motion, more freedom to move around the kit.

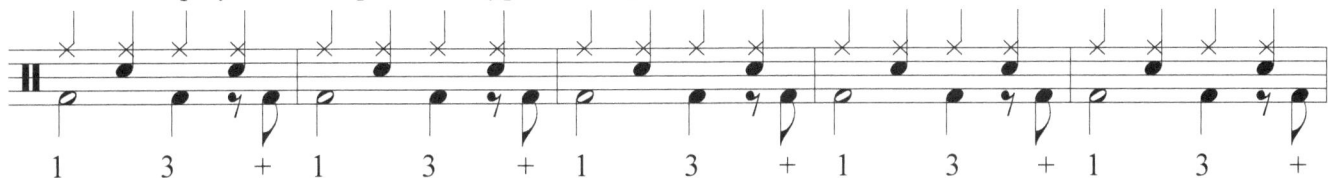

Ride Cymbal

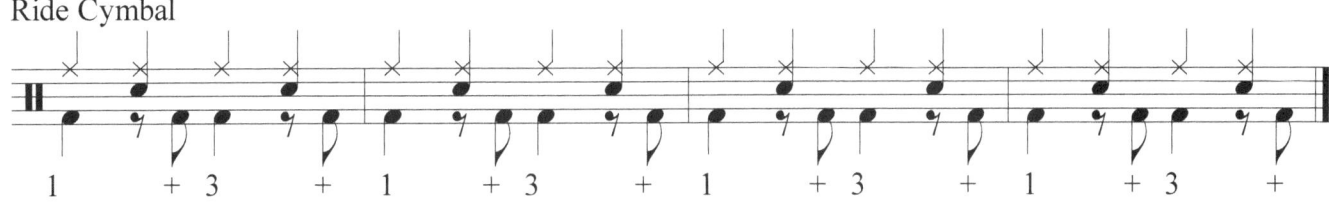

8TH NOTE RHYTHMS

Welcome guys, to the brand new 8th note rhythm beats section. This page opens up a whole new type of drumming for you. We are now doubling our qtr note beats to 8th notes on the high-hat

Now lets try the 8th note off beat rhythms on the kick drum. Remember to count your high hat as 1+2+3+4+

Lets try 3 different bars in a row with added crash cymbal on the one count.

8TH NOTE ACCENTS

Welcome to the 8th note accents, the little arrow looking sign on top of a note shows you an accent sign. With an accent, we want to hit that note louder than a non-accented note, hence we get a dynamically louder softer feel to our playing.

Ok guys getting a little harder now, remember to keep counting our 8th notes as 1+2+3+4+
And making sure to get that nice accented sound happening on the snare drum.

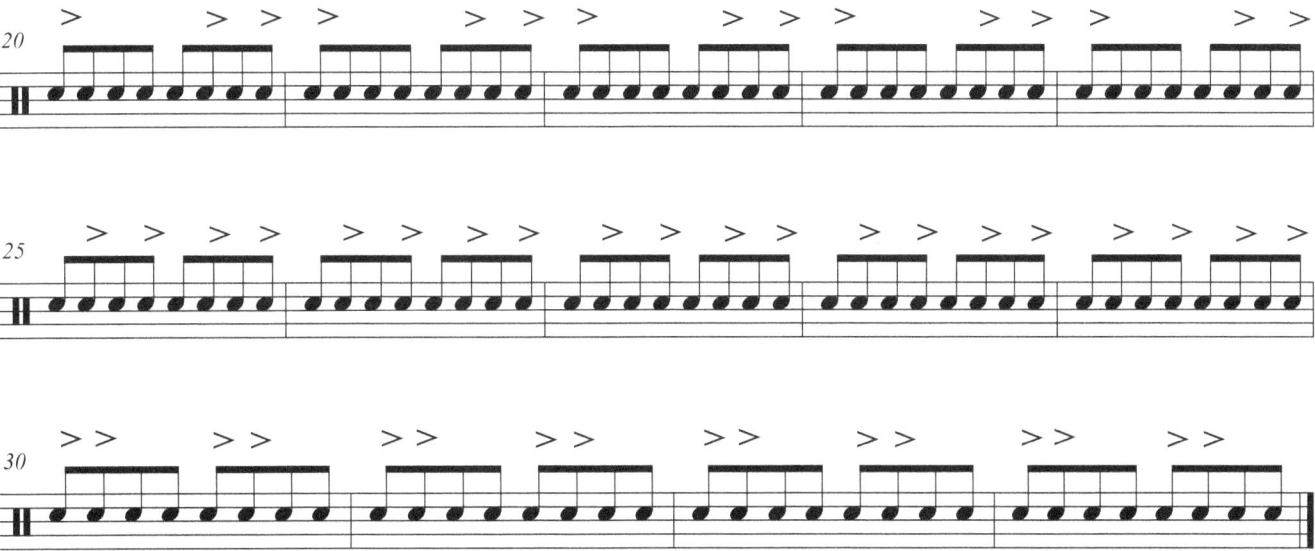

THE DRUM HUB

8TH NOTE ACCENTS ON TOMS

Just remember guys certain accents will make you alternate from your left to right

Side note remember our note stems can face up or down on the staff lines.
Just focus on where the note is placed on the staff line, **see above.**

8TH NOTE RHYTHMS WITH QUARTER AND 8TH ROLLS

We now have 8th note rhythm sections with a rolls on the snare. We are using mixed combination of qtrs and 8th on the snare. Be sure to count out loud and take your time with your timing.

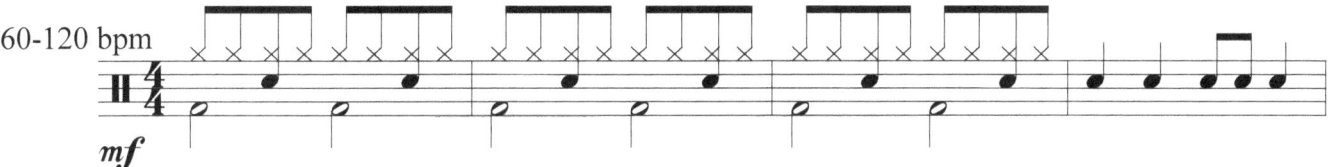

Hopefully by now we should be able to play without the help of the numbers, good luck!

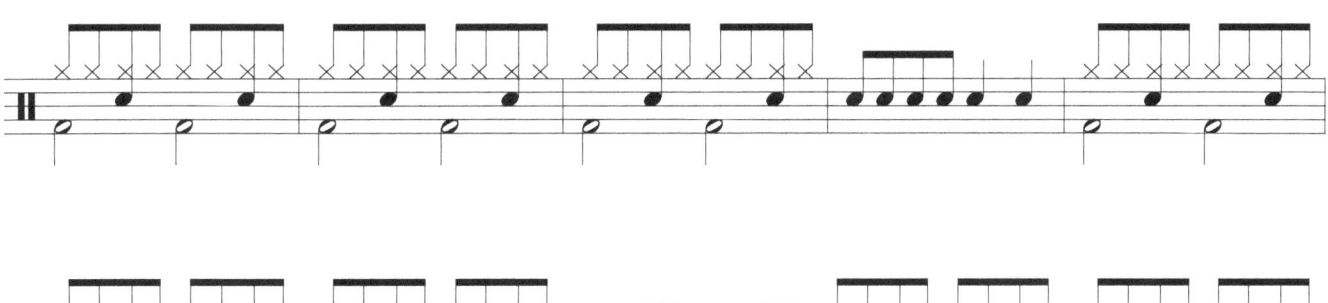

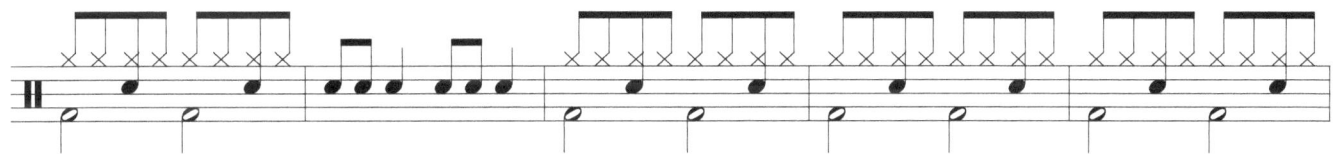

If you're finding this exercise quite easy, try speeding it up. Have fun!

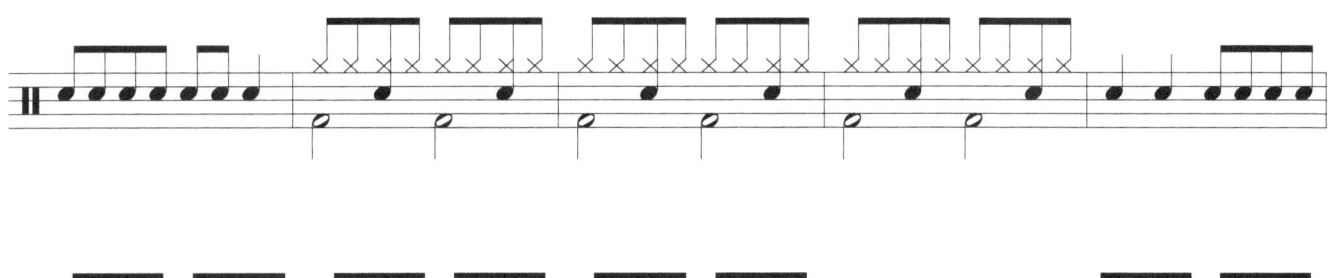

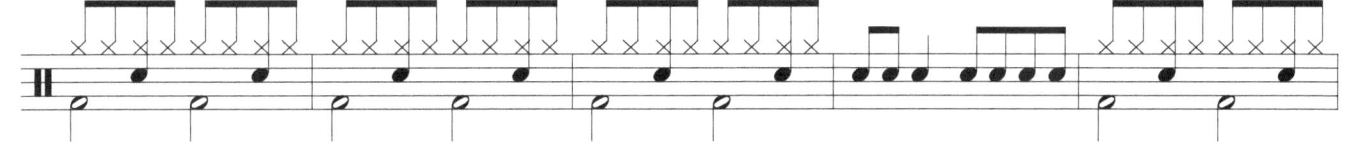

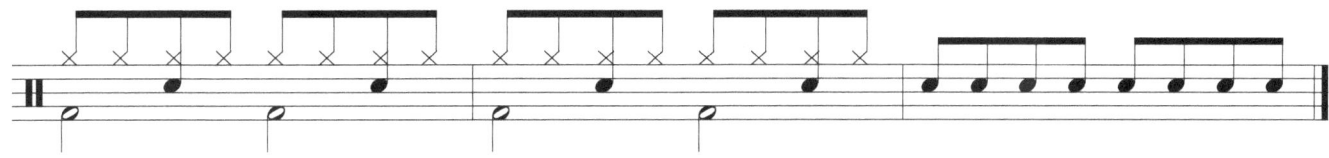

THE DRUM HUB

MIXED NOTE COMBINATIONS ON TOMS

Now we have mixed qtrs and 8th note combinations on our tom rolls. Remember to look closely at your staff lines and hit the correct toms, go slowly and count out loud.

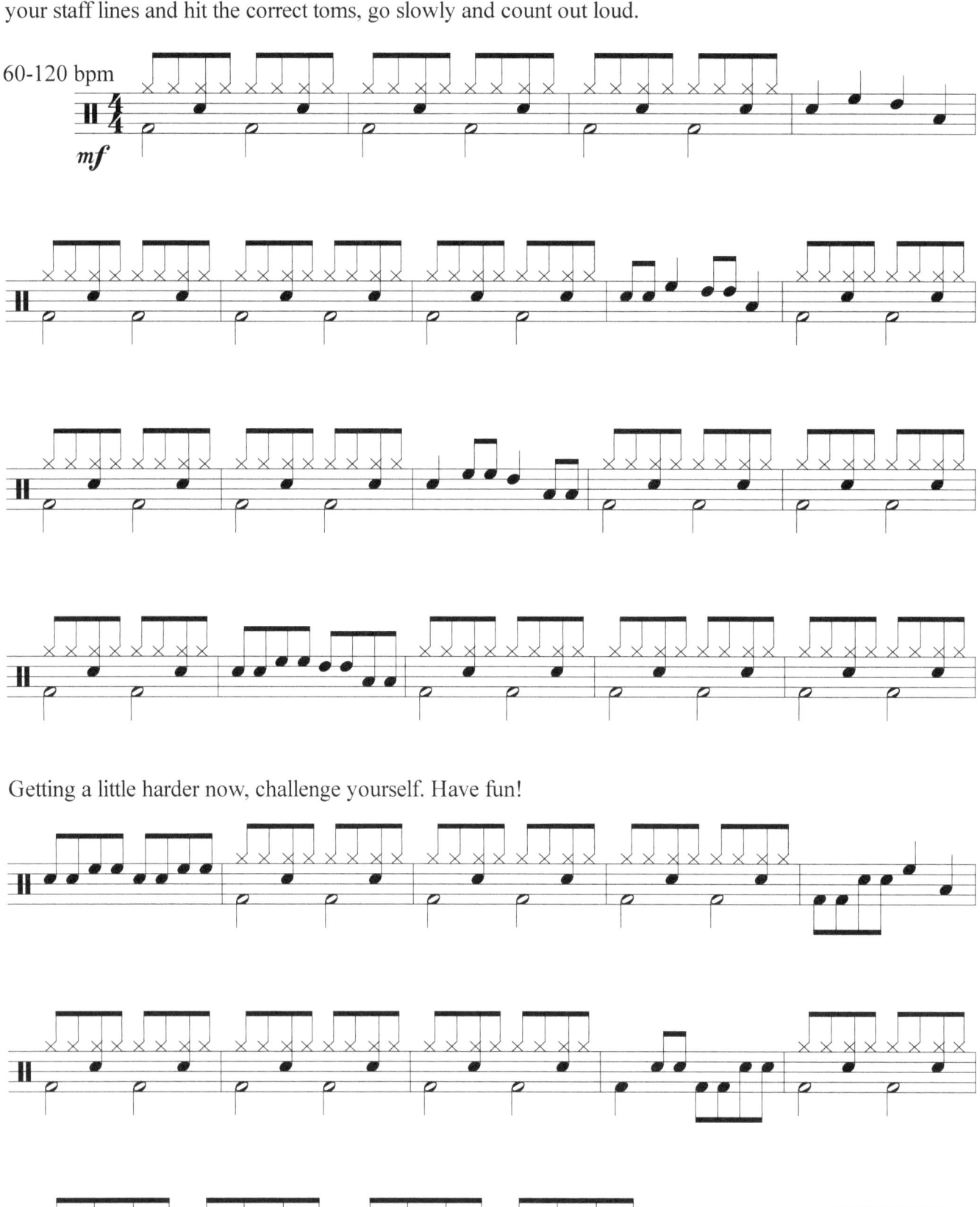

Getting a little harder now, challenge yourself. Have fun!

QUARTER AND 8TH NOTE COMBINATION STUDY

In this combination study, we are using all of our notes and rests that we have learnt so far in chapter #2
Remember to count slowly and work out your rolls.

Always study your staff lines and remember to hit your correct snares and toms.

THE DRUM HUB

QUARTER AND 8TH NOTE TRANSISTIONS

Ok guys on this page we want to transition our qtr note rhythms into our 8th note rhythms without stopping. Notice they are in brackets, try each bracket section separately. The kick patterns are the same, but you will double your notes on the high-hat on each transition. Good luck!

SYNCOPATION PART #1

Ok guys, we now have a technique called Syncopation. This a musical technique involving the accentuation of a normally weak beat or offbeat in a rhythm. It adds a dynamic and unexpected element to the music, creating a sense of groove and rhythm complexity. Remember to go slow and work out the distances of our notes.

Notice bar **1**, **2** and **3** are written different but will sound the same. When you see a tie from one note to another, you will skip that note it is tied too

8TH NOTE SYNCOPATED SNARE RHYTHMS

Hey guys, the most basic rhythms are played with the snare on 2 and 4, there's no reason why we can't move the snare off the 2 and 4 count, to give us a nice **syncopated** feel, this will change our standard rhythm sound.

Getting harder now, remember to go slow and count out loud.

8TH NOTE OFF BEAT RHYTHMS

Welcome to your 8th note off beat rhythm page, this is a fun way to play your off beats. This will give you a disco beat type feel on the high hat. Remember the 8th note rest on your high hat line.

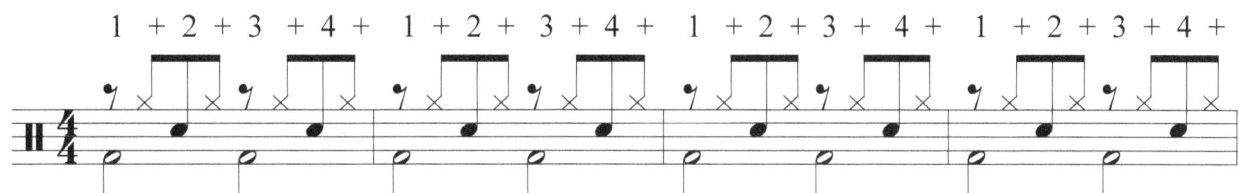

Notice the rhythm above, we have rested all of our primary numbers, hence we only play the + of the 8th note rhytms. In return, it gives a nice off beat feel.

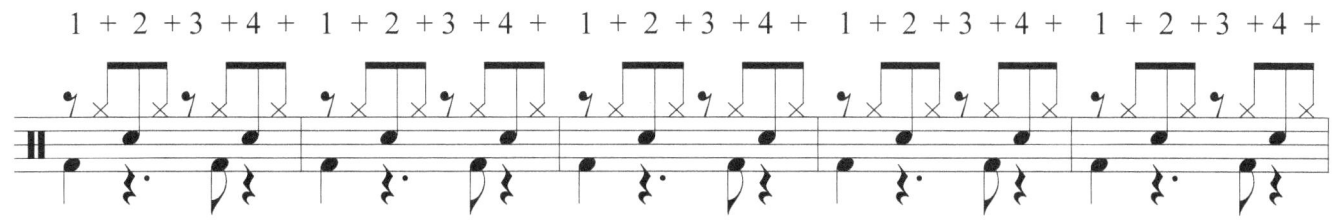

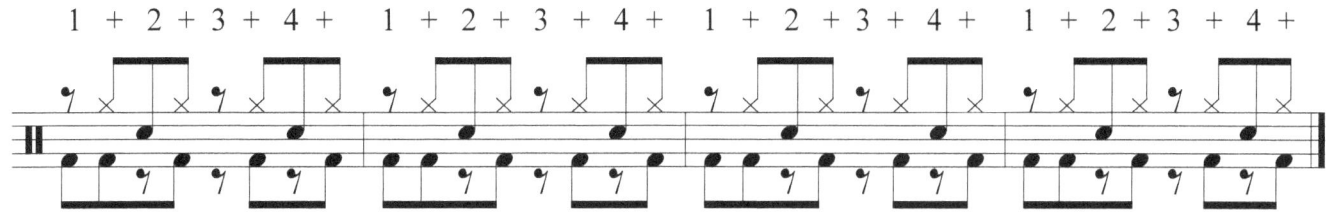

8th Note High Hat Exercises

Welcome to getting four parts of your body moving at once, you will open handed on this section, allowing to get your high hat chip. Remember to go slow and get that qtr note chip on your left foot on every primary number. This will aid us in keeping perfect timing, good luck and do your best.

Ride cymbol

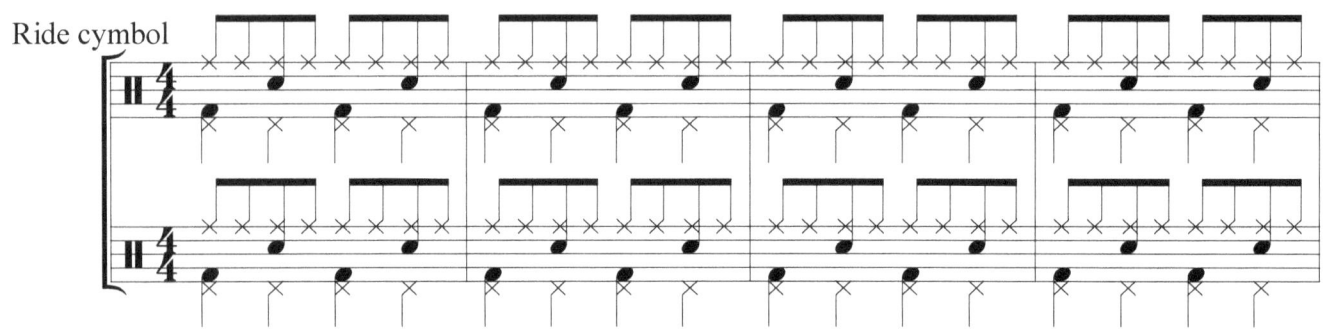

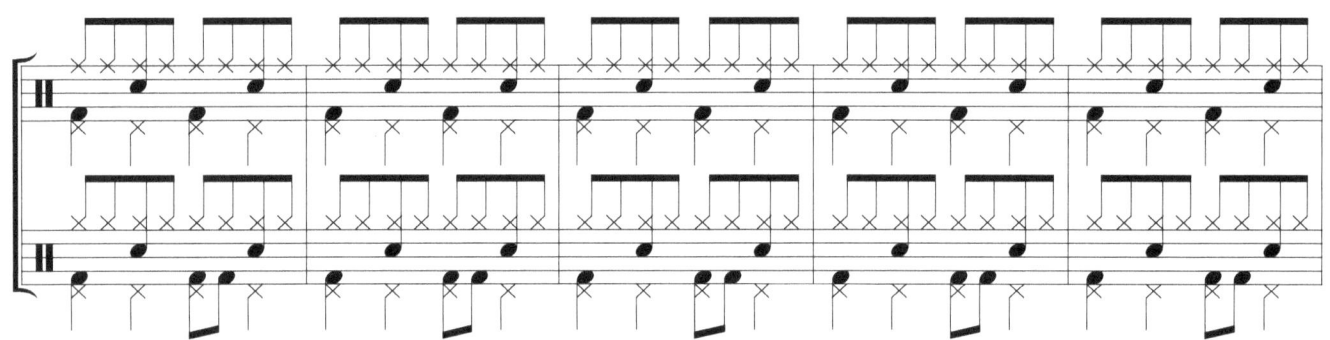

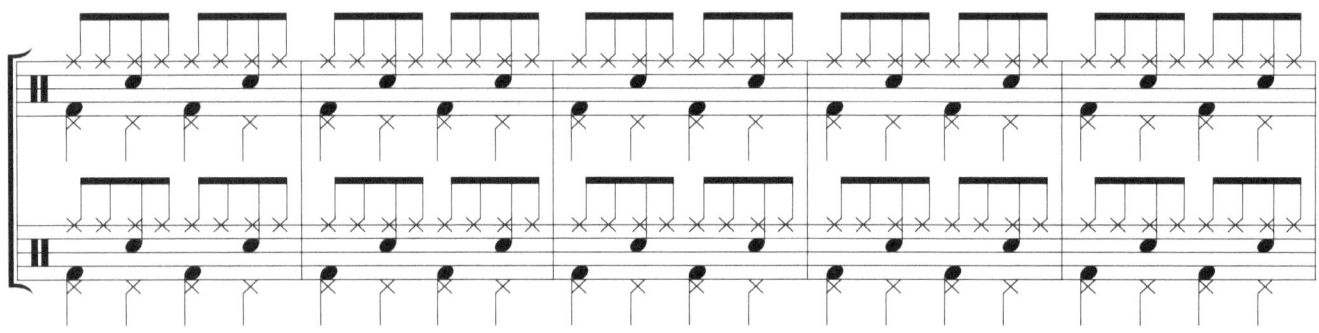

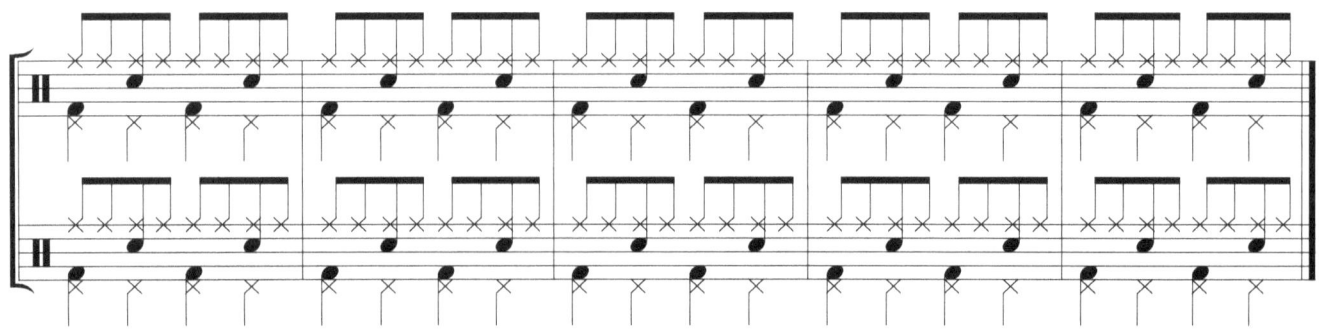

SKILL TESTER #2

Welcome to the end of **chapter 2**. Lets test our learning with this mixed qtr and 8th note rhythm section, look for your crash cymbals, mixed notes and rests. Have fun and remember to count out loud.

What are these notes you might ask? Welcome to chapter 3.

THE DRUM HUB

SOLO EXERCISE

Well done guys for completing chapter 2. In this solo section we are going to introduce the Cresendo ―――――― This means your playing will become gradually louder.

Decresendo ―――――― This means your playing will gradually become quieter.

STUDENT PRACTICAL SUMMARY

On these blank staff lines use your bars to practise writing down the notation that you have learnt thus far. Try adding in your rests and write out some of your favourite rhythms. Have fun!

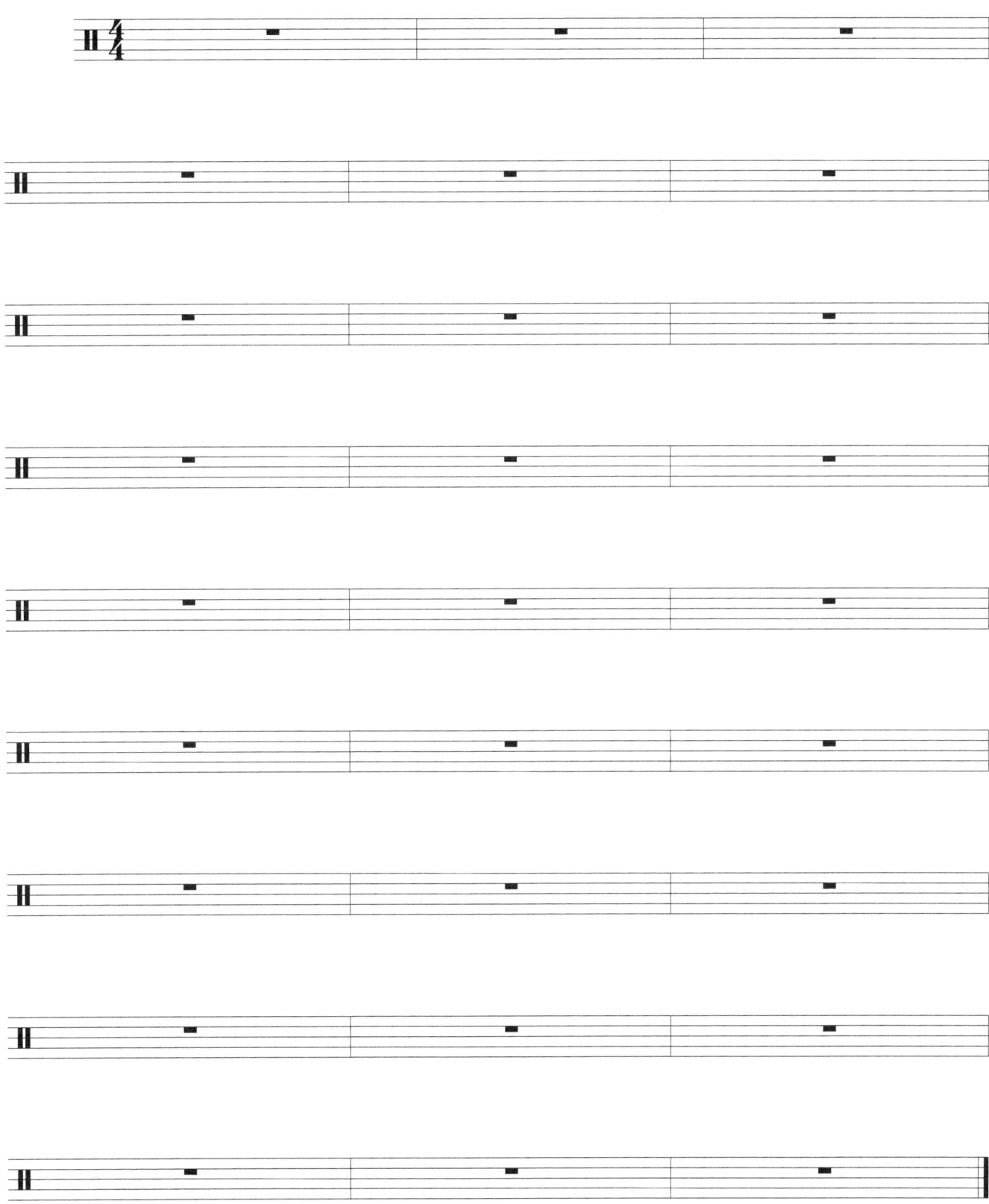

Chapter 3

UNDERSTANDING THE 16TH NOTE

Congratulations, welcome to chapter 3. Now we can step it up a bit, on this page we are going to learn how to divide two 8th notes into four 16th notes. Doubling the count from 1+2+3+4+ to
1e+a 2e+a 3e+a 4e+a

So remember how to count the 8th note. We can indetify the 8th note by the one horizontal beam tail, which joins the 2 notes together.

As you can see our brand new 16th notes have 2 horizontal lines joining the notes together, these beam tails are very important to remember.

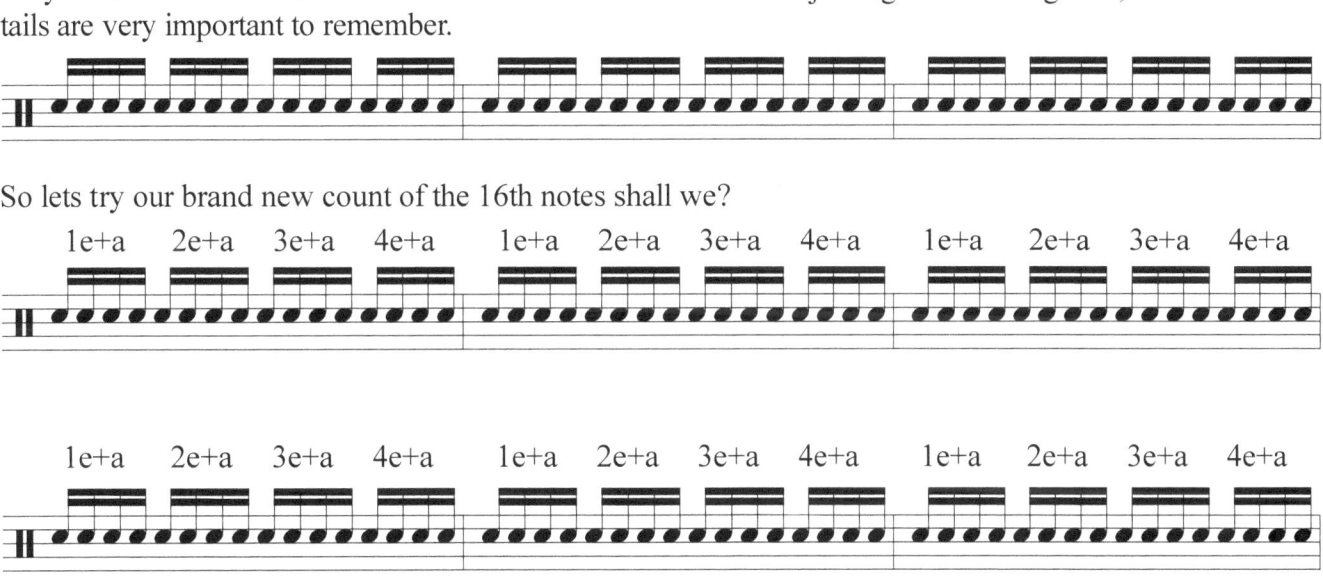

So lets try our brand new count of the 16th notes shall we?

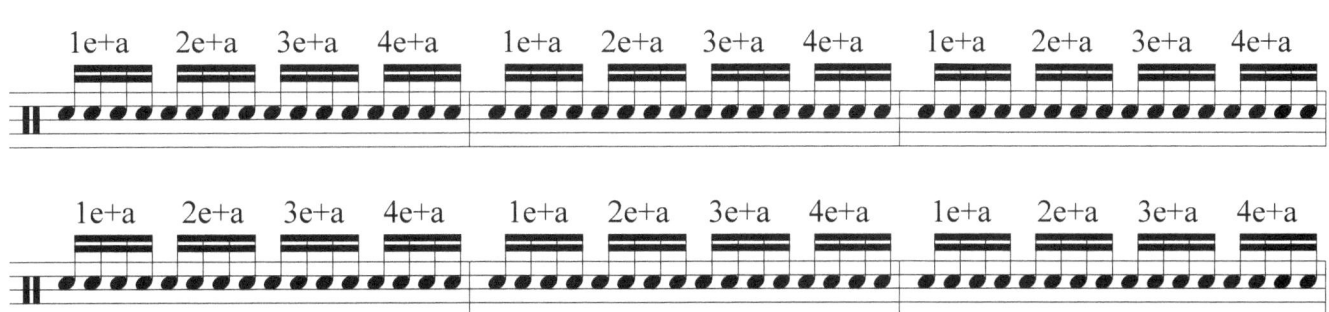

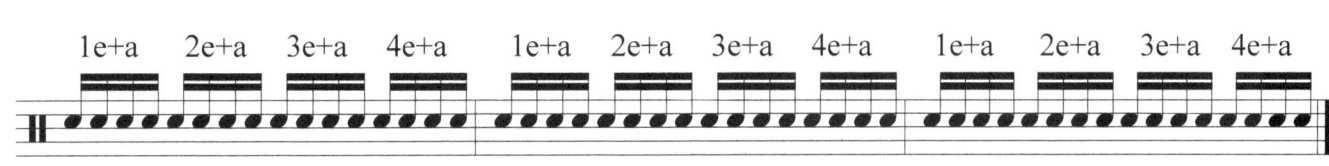

THE DRUM HUB 45

QUARTER 16TH ON SNARE

Lets have fun mixing our qtrs and 16th notes on our snare, remember to count our brand new 16th note as 1e+a 2e+a 3e+a 4e+a. Take it slow and count out loud.

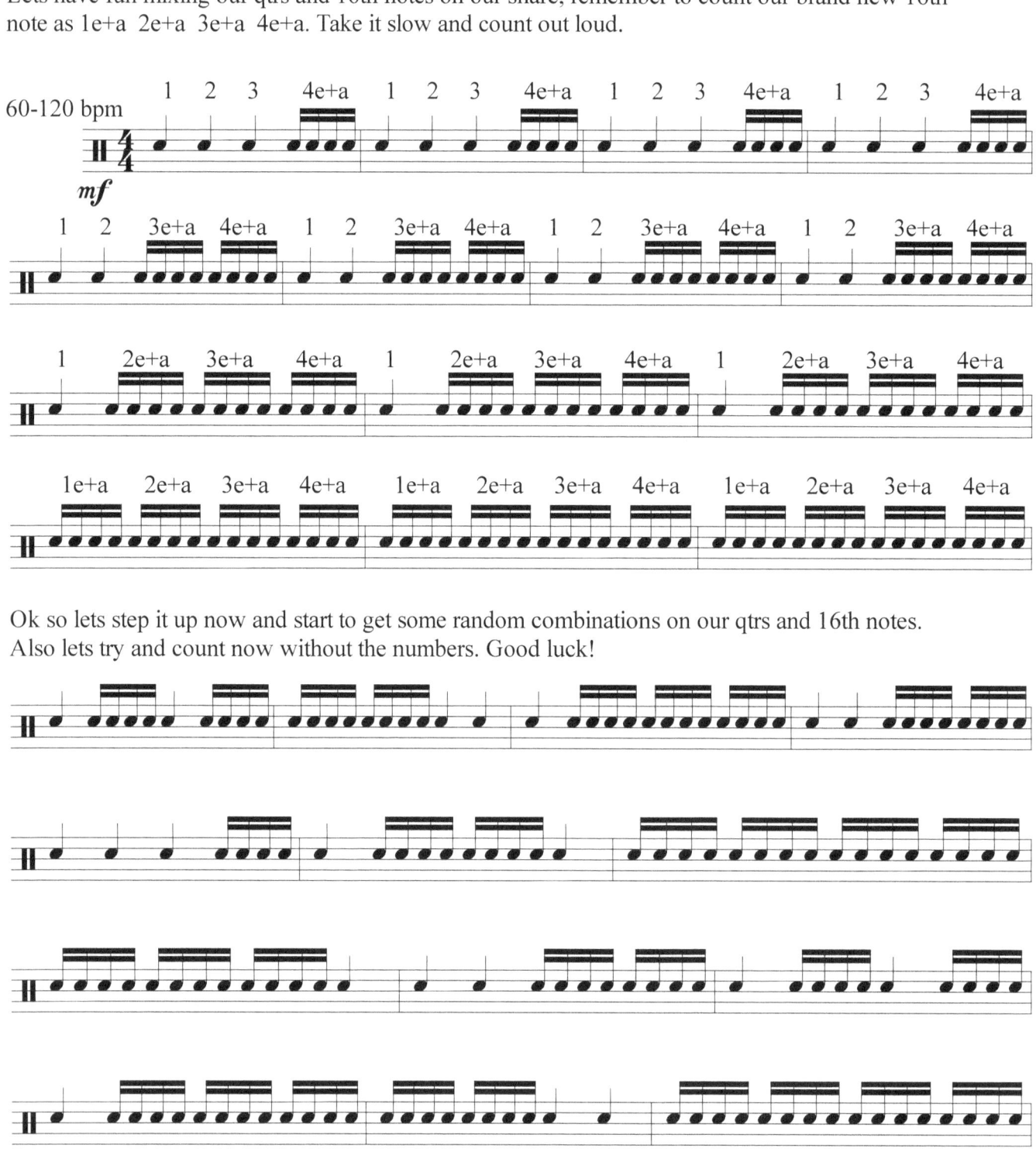

Ok so lets step it up now and start to get some random combinations on our qtrs and 16th notes. Also lets try and count now without the numbers. Good luck!

8TH 16TH ON SNARE

Lets try our new 8th and 16th notes together on the snare. Remembering to count
1+2+3+4+ and 1e+a 2e+a 3e+a 4e+a

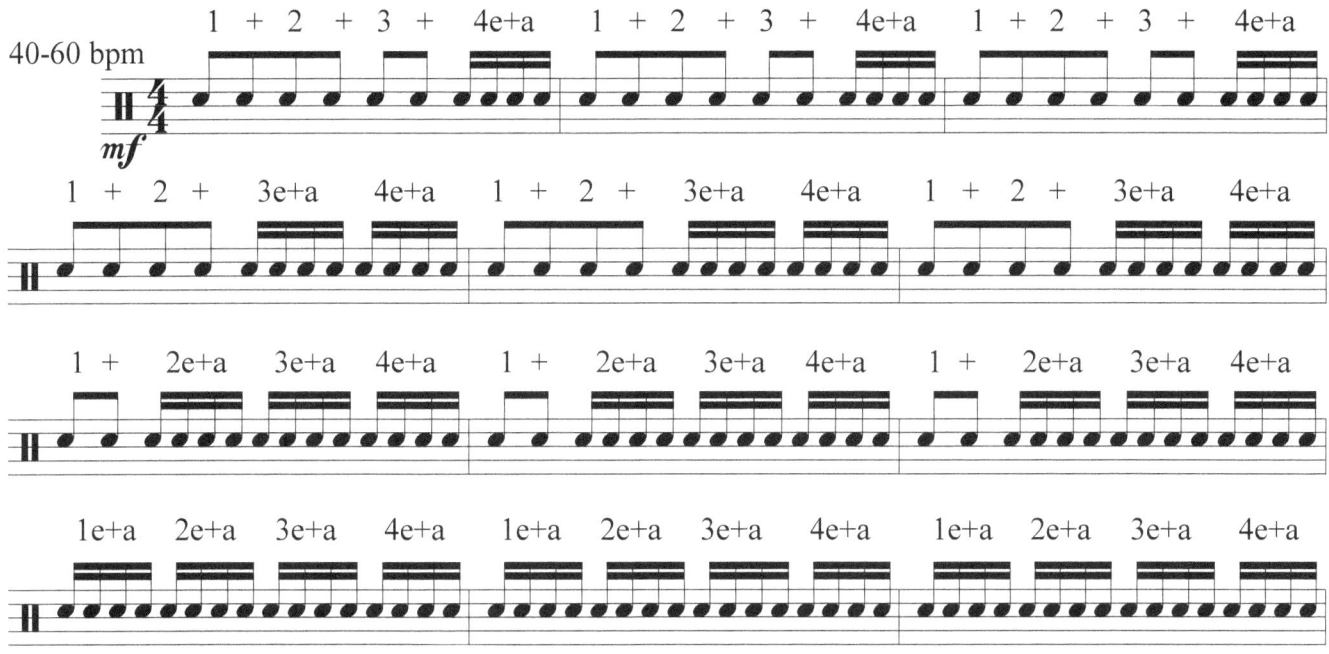

Ok once again lets step it up to get our random 8th and 16th combinations in on the snare.
lets test ourselves and try without the numbers.

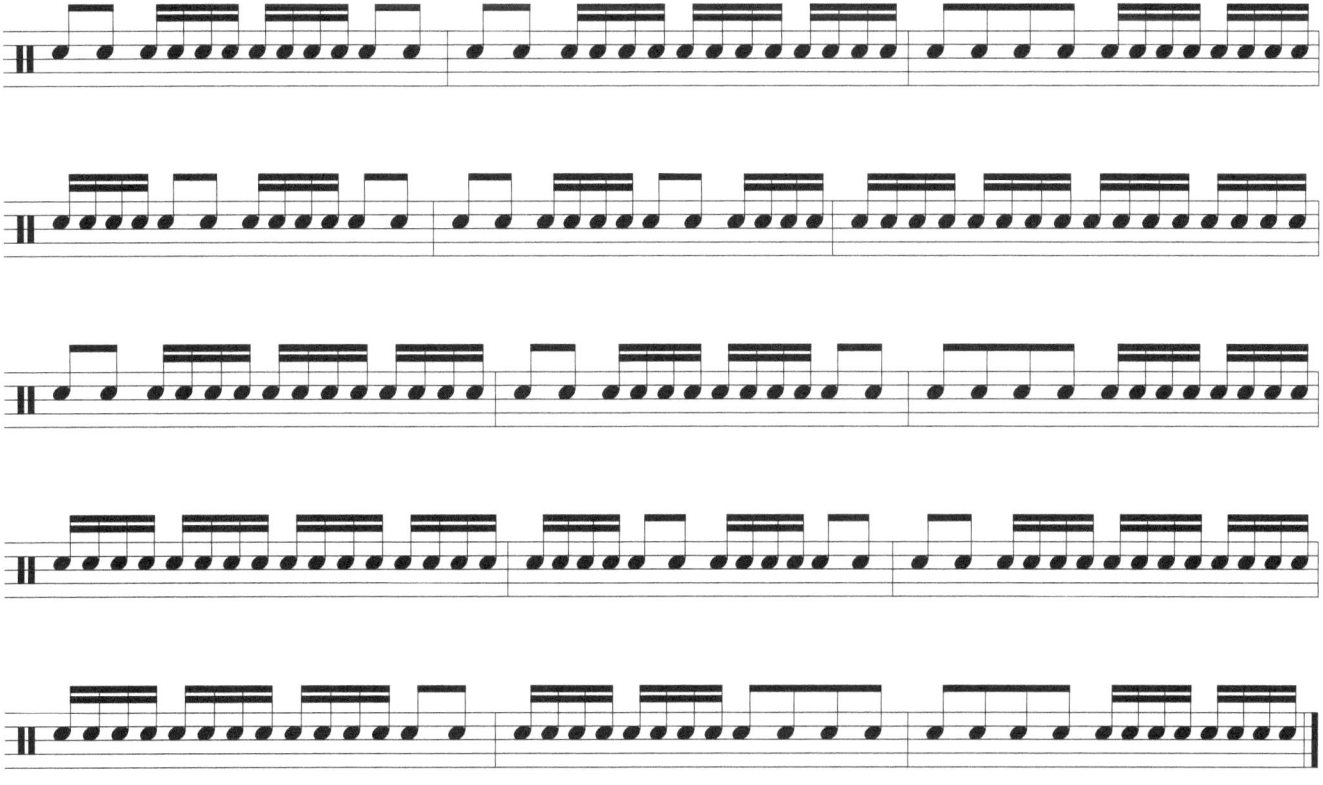

16TH NOTE ACCENTS

Just like our 8th note accents in previous chapter, try the 16th accents now, these are a lot of fun to play. Just remember to start off slow and get a nice dynamic feel with your accents Enjoy!

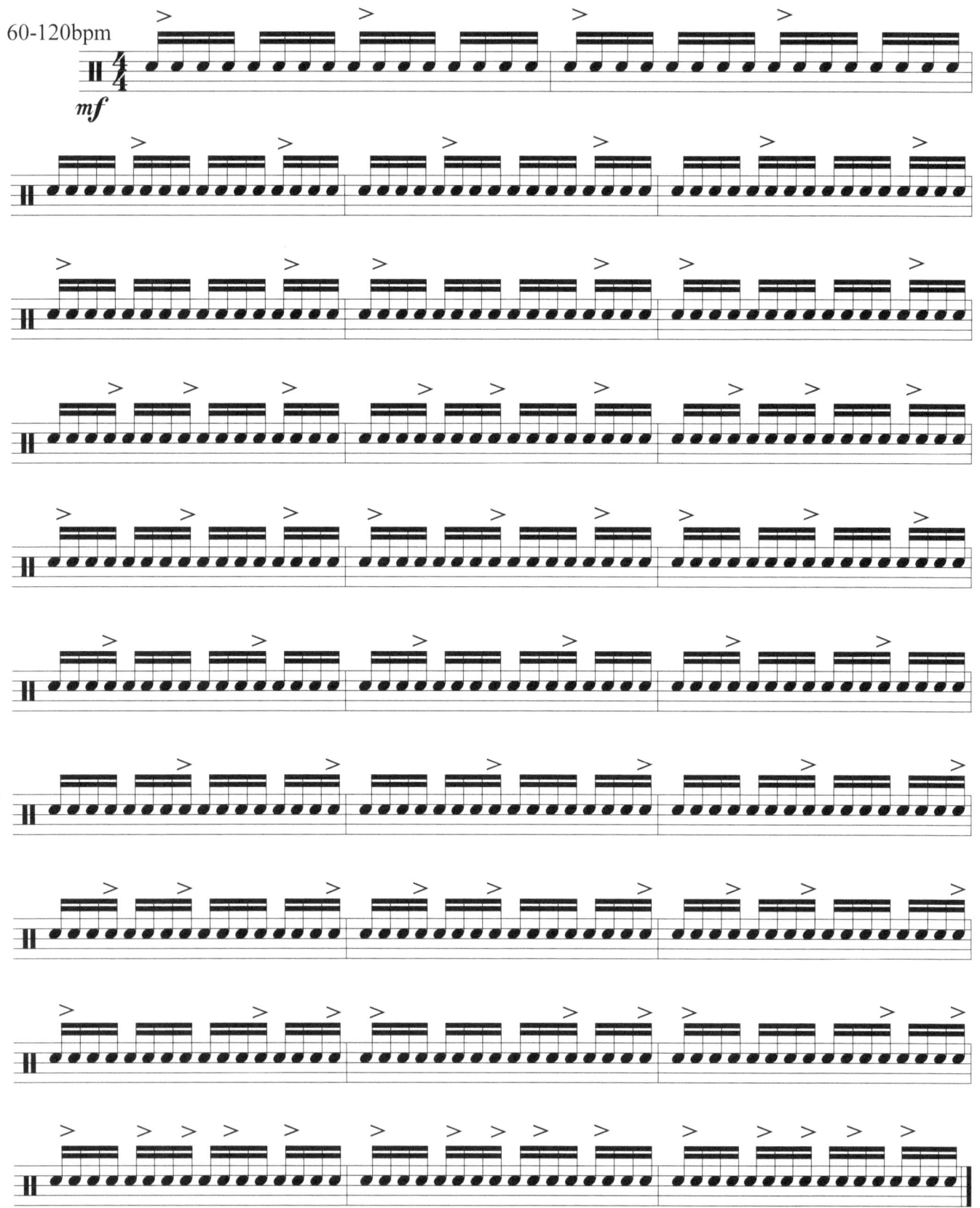

1 e + a 2 e + a 3 e + a 4 e + a

Bring this last accented rhythm up to **Allegro** 110-130 bpm tempo it's a lot of fun to play.

QUARTER 8TH 16TH ON SNARE WITH FOOT

Lets enjoy this mixed note combination exercise. Now we are going to combine all our qtrs, 8th, 16th notes together on our snare and use our qtr note foot as our metronome to keep us in time. Remember to always count out loud. Have fun!

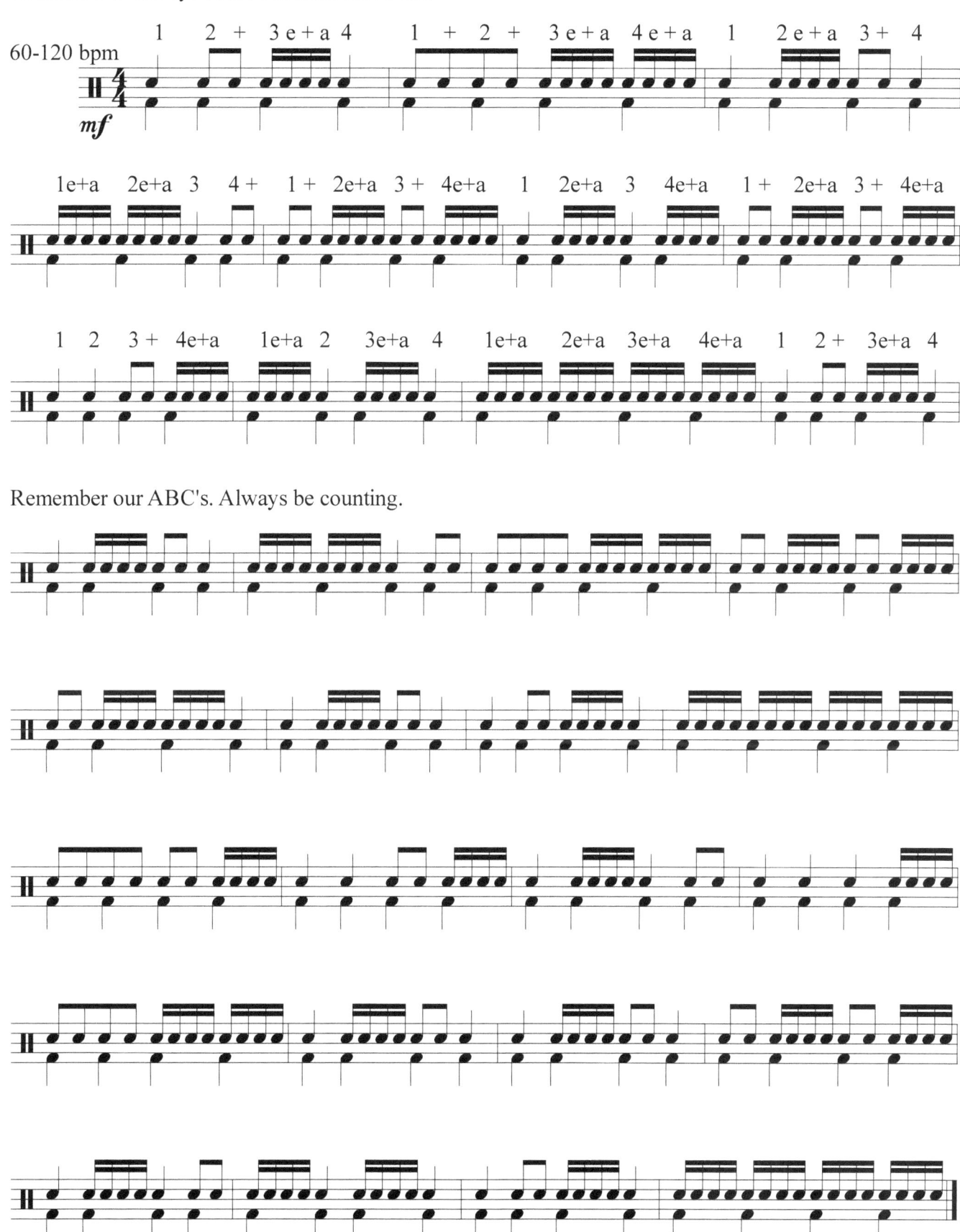

Remember our ABC's. Always be counting.

UNDERSTANDING THE 16 NOTE REST

Just like in chapter 2, learning the 8th note rest, we are moving onto the 16th note rest. Notice how the 16th note rests has two rest tails to match the two beam tails on the 16th note. These are very important, they identify our rests to our rightful note.

1 e + a 2 e + a 3 e + a 4 e + a

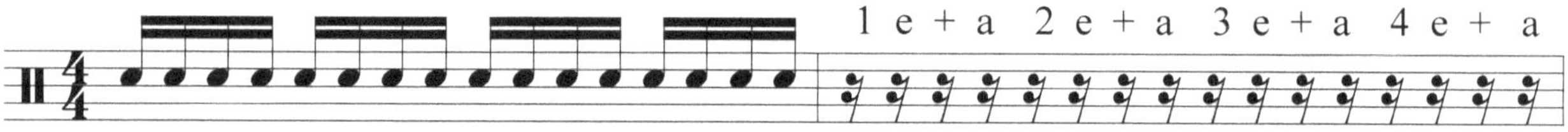

1 e + a 2 e + a 3 e + a 4 e + a

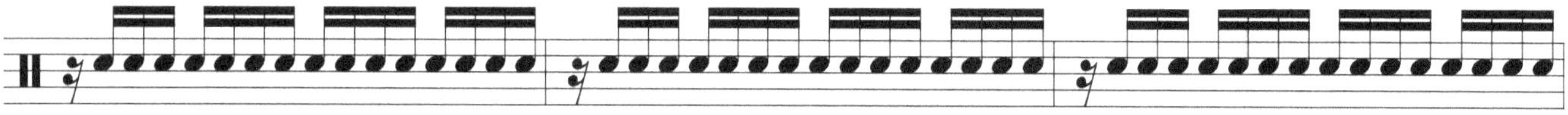

1 **e** + a 2 e + a 3 e + a 4 e + a

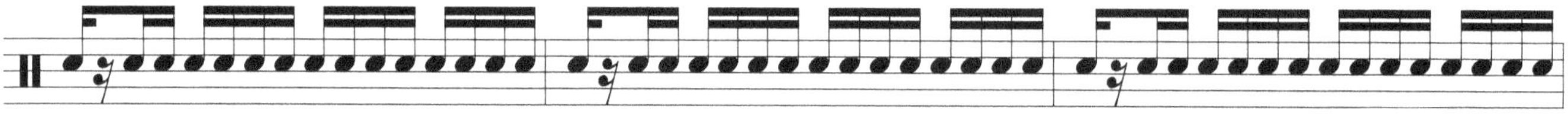

1 e + a 2 e + a 3 e + a 4 e + a

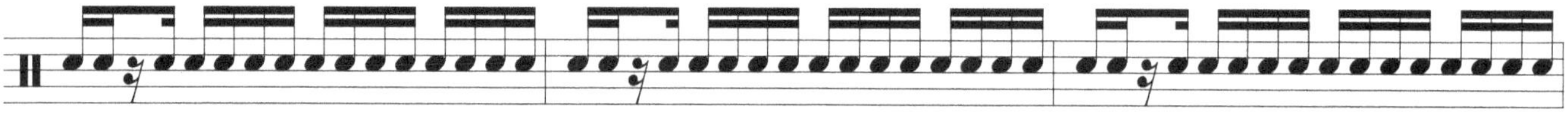

1 e + **a** 2 e + a 3 e + a 4 e + a

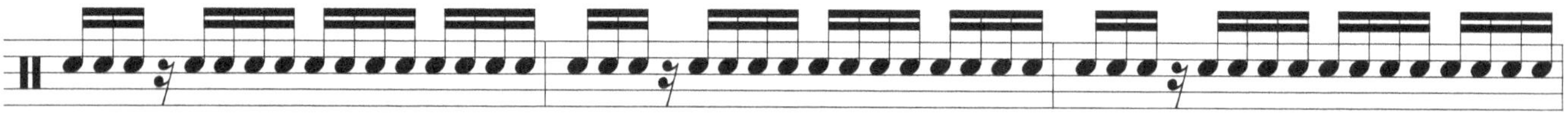

Ok now lets try our random 16th note rests. Start off slow and get more creative, remember to count out loud. Do the best you can.

1 e + a 2 e + a 3 e + a 4 e + a 1 e + a 2 e + a 3 e + a 4 e + a 1 e + a 2 e + a 3 e + a 4 e + a

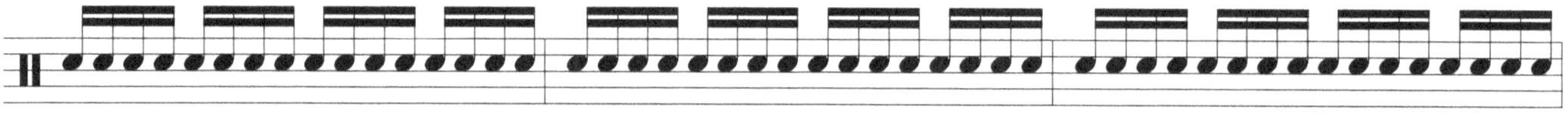

1 e + a 2 e + a 3 e + a 4 e + a 1 e + a 2 e + a 3 e + a 4 e + a 1 e + a 2 e + a 3 e + a 4 e + a

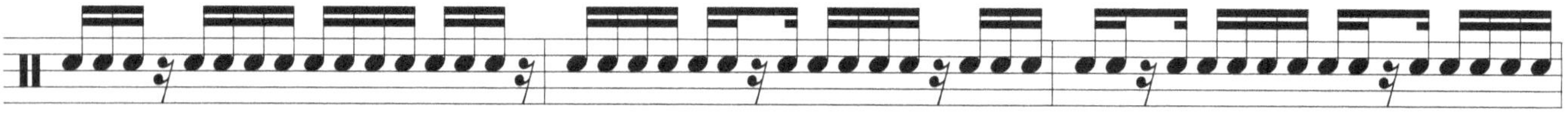

Ok lets try it without using our numbers, go slow and enjoy.

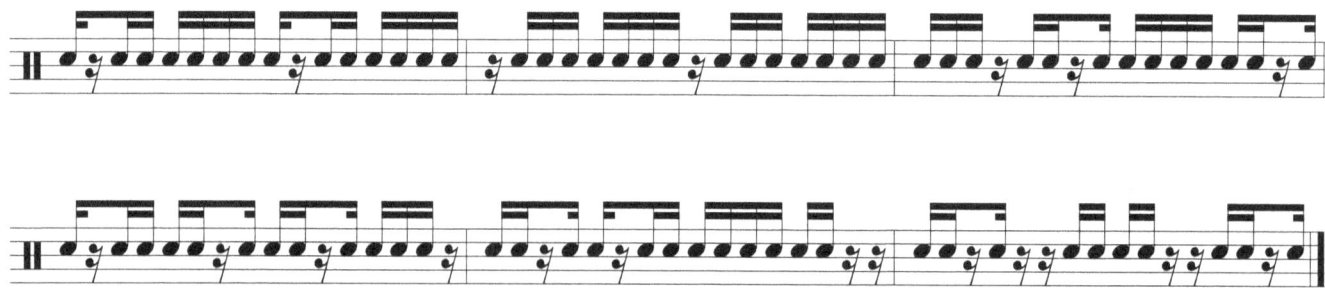

MIXED NOTES AND REST CHALLENGE

In this mixed note and rest exercise, we are going to study the notes and their accompanied rests, and how there applied to one another. Remember to focus on their beam tails to correctly identify each rest and partnered note.

Ok now lets go really slow and count without the numbers. Feel free to use your kick drum on the qtr notes as your metronome. Good luck!

16TH NOTE RHYTHMS WITH SNARE COMBINATIONS

Welcome to the 16th note rhythm page. Remember just like the qtr and 8th rhythms on the high-hat, theres no reason why we can't play 16th's the same way. Remember to count 1e+a's on your high-hat and keep your kick on the 1 and 3.

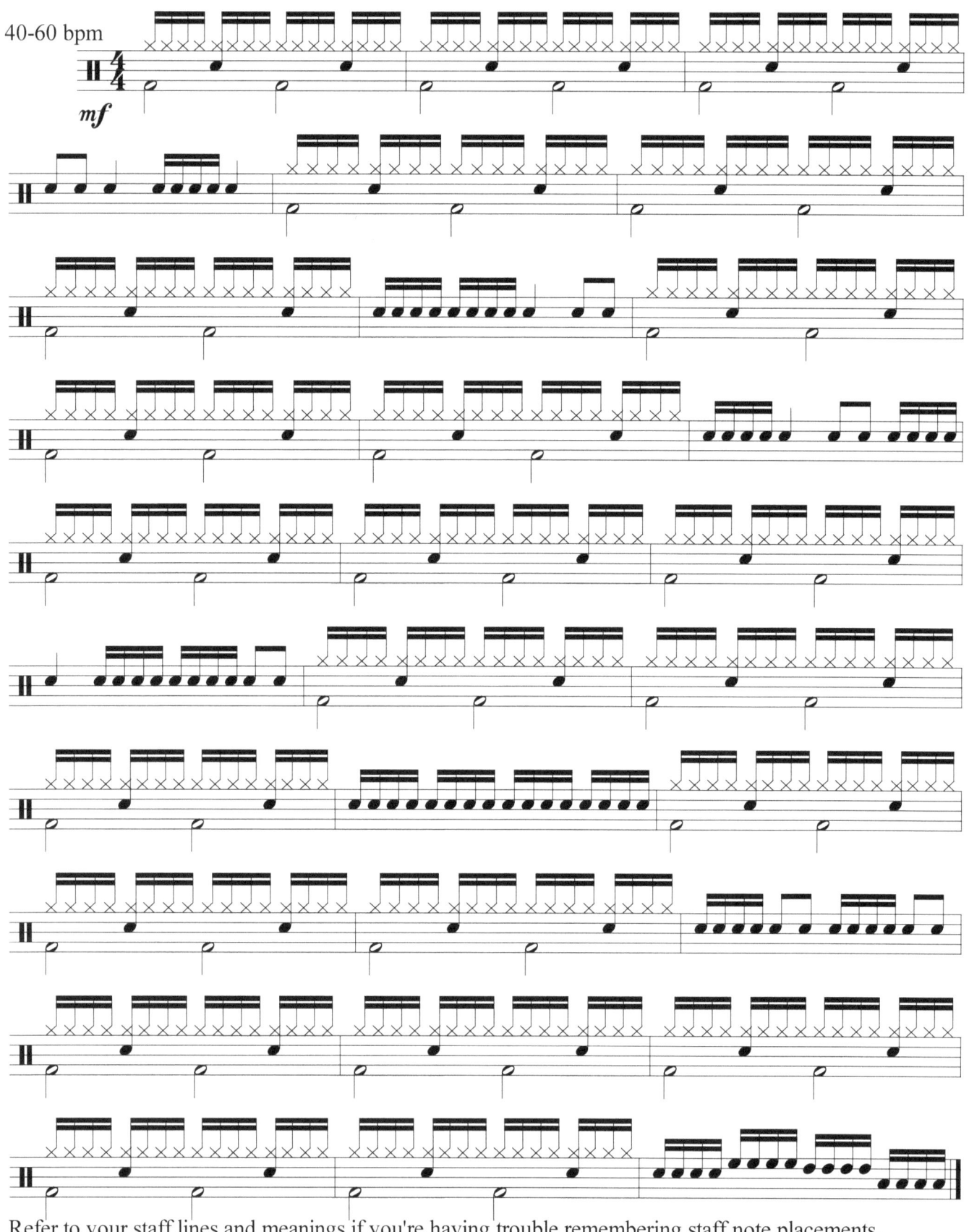

Refer to your staff lines and meanings if you're having trouble remembering staff note placements.

16TH NOTE RHYTHMS WITH SNARE TOM COMBINATIONS

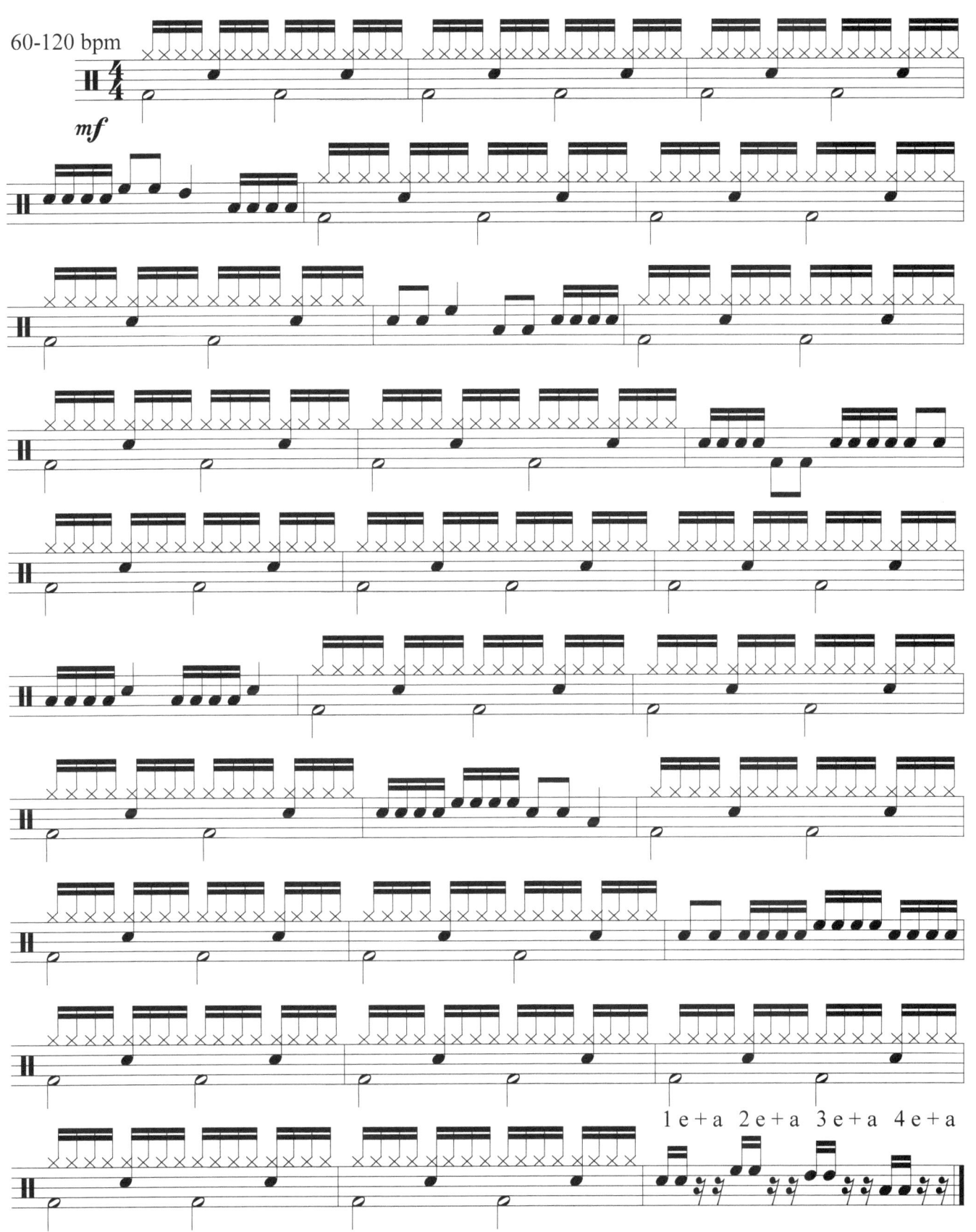

Side note, remember to count your rests in this complex roll.

16TH NOTE ACCENTS ON TOMS

Just remember guys, it does not matter which way our note stems are facing it can be up or down on the staff lines. It's very important to see which line the note is placed in on the staff line, to allocate which drum to hit.

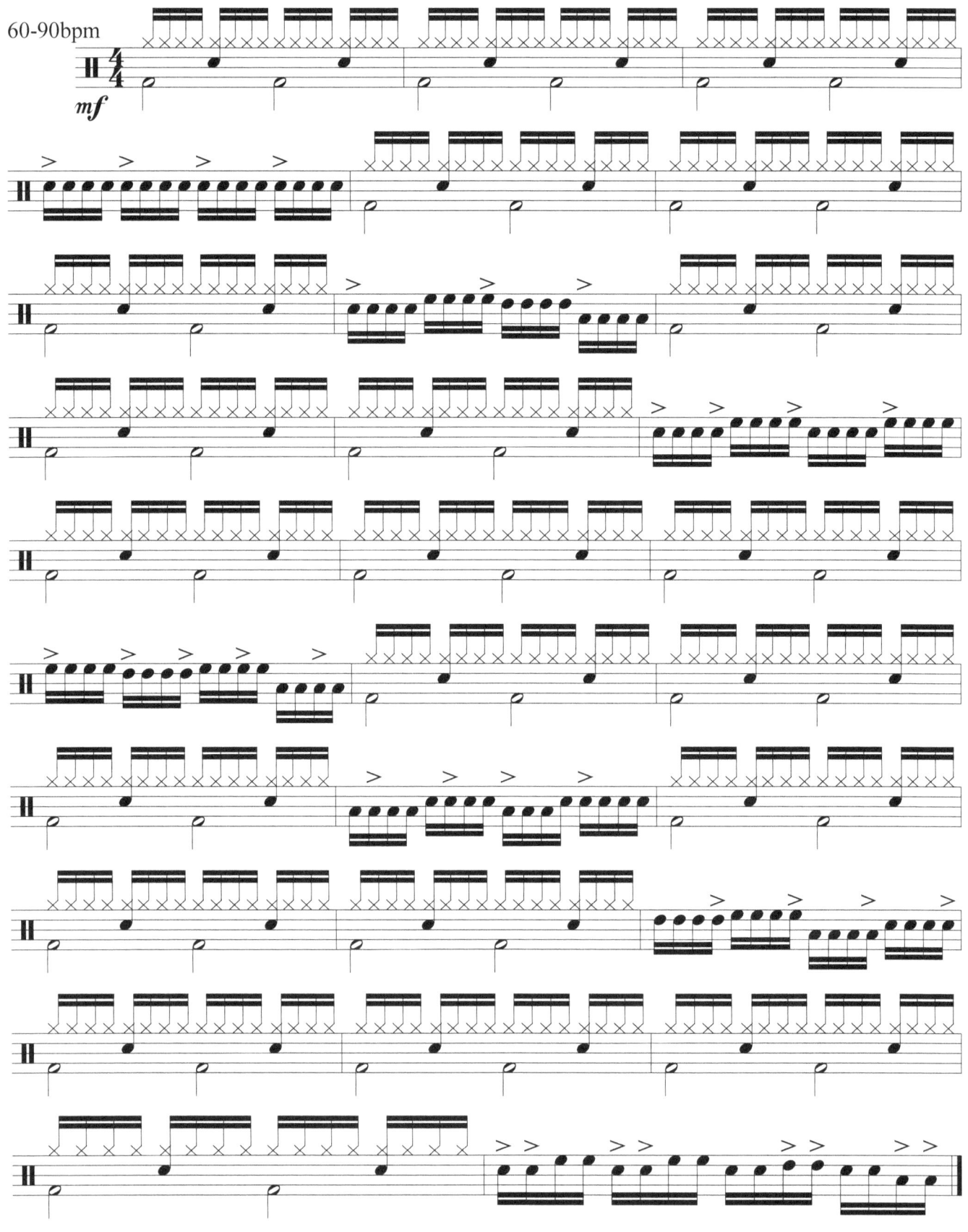

16TH NOTE RHYTHMS WITH TOM ROLLS AND RESTS

We are really rolling along now guys, these are very complex 16th note rolls. Remember to count all your 16th notes and rests together, count them slowly as 1e+a etc. Remember to count all information in the bar, I have given you some examples.

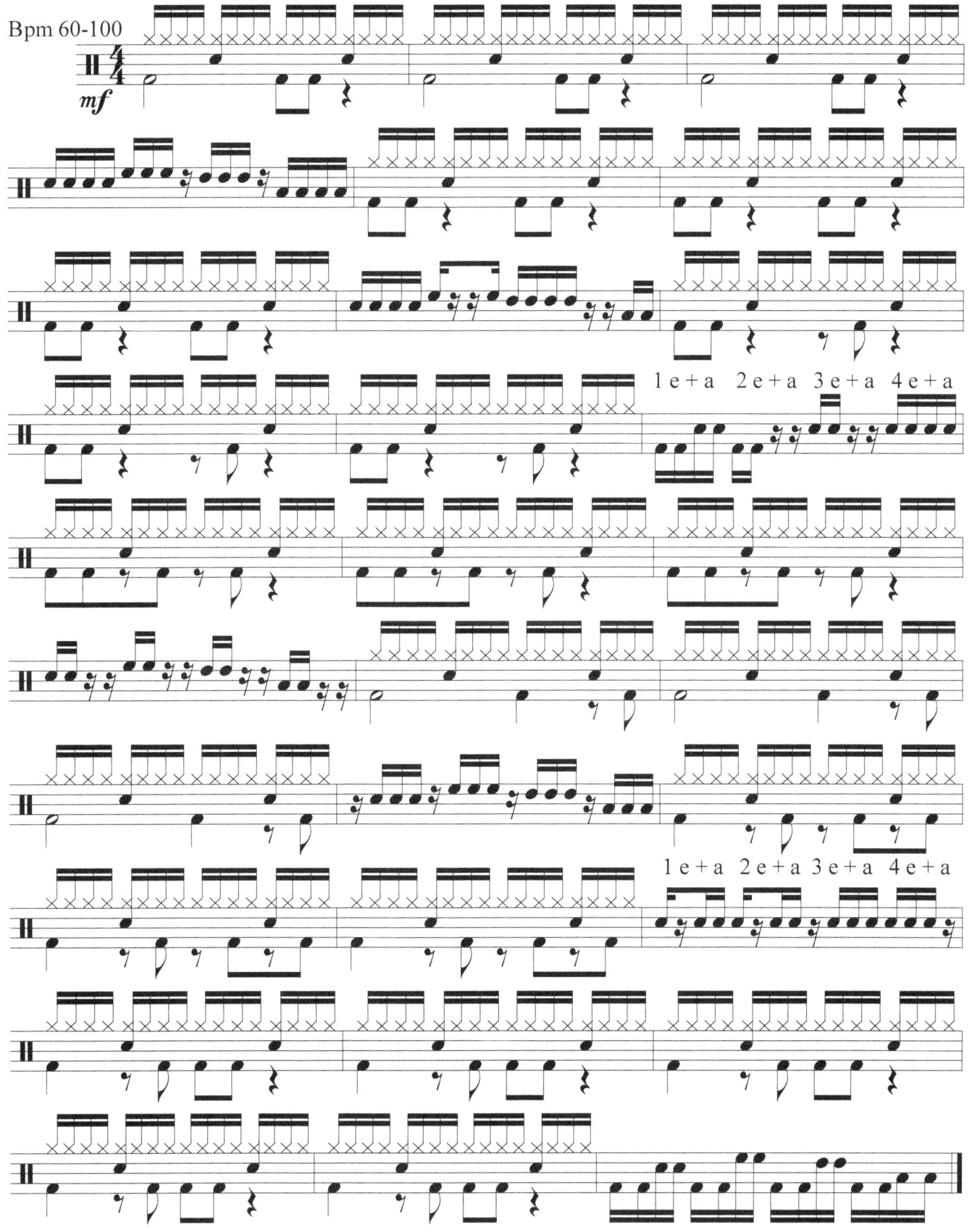

SOLO EXERCISE

Ok guys in the solo section we our introducing our (single) and (double) bar repeat sign.
A single repeat sign looks like a thin vertical line with two dots either side (as pictured below)
The double bar repeat sign is similar but will be denote with a number 2 on top indicating to go back
and play the previous two bars. Good luck, these solo are getting a bit more advanced now.

STUDENT PRACTICAL SUMMARY

On these blank staff lines use you're bars to practise writing down the notation that you have learnt thus far. Try adding in your rests and write out some of your favourite rhythms. Enjoy the process.

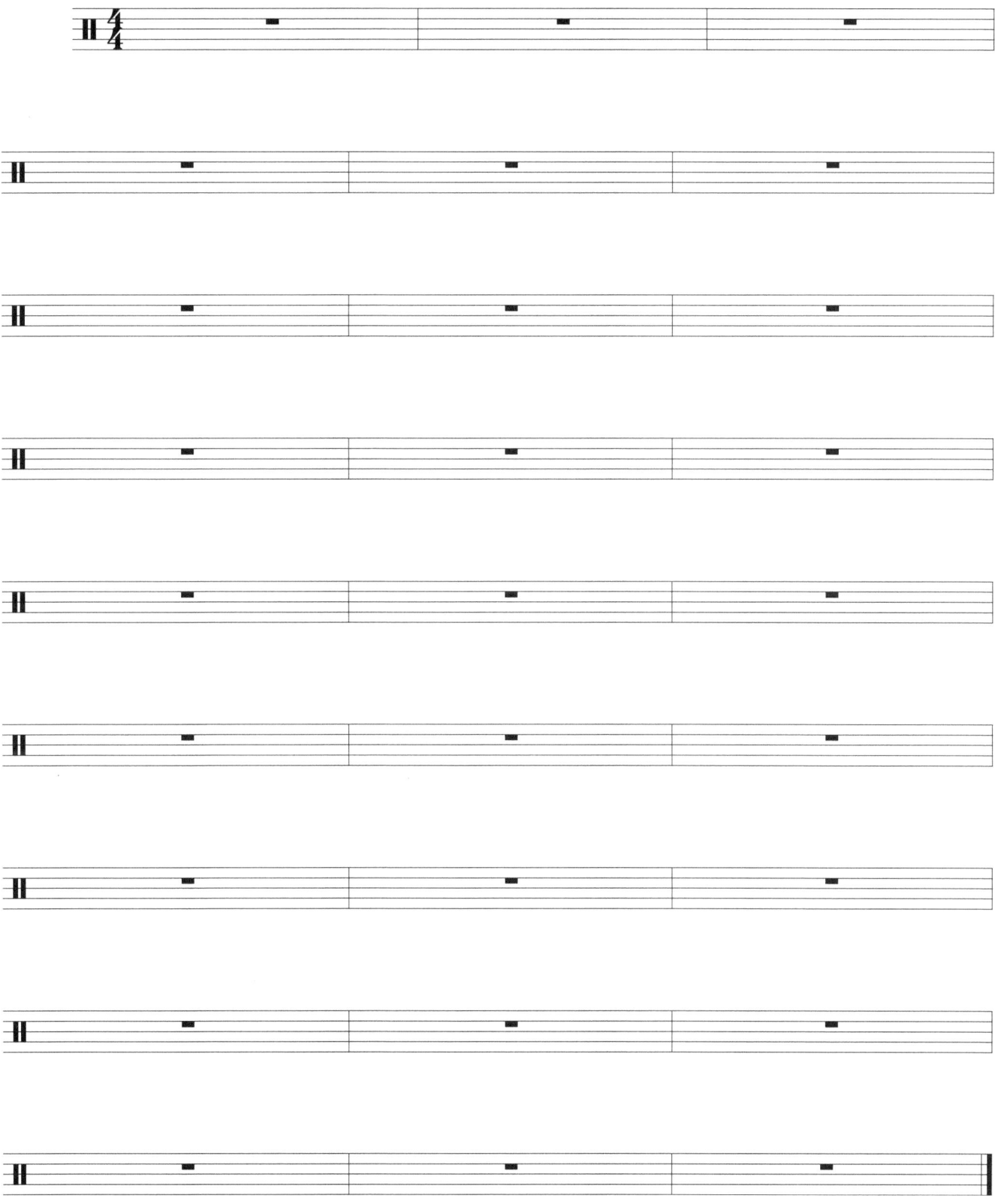

THE DRUM HUB

Chapter 4

DOTTED NOTES AND 16TH NOTE VARIATIONS

Ok guys, welcome to the dotted note. With the dotted note we need to divide the original notes value into two halves and add half again. In other words 1.5 x the note. This will extend the notes distance by 50%, all dotted notes will equal 3 notes in total.

THE DRUM HUB

DOTTED NOTE AND SYNCOPATION PART #2

Welcome to part #2 of syncopation. We are going to add in the dotted quarter note in this exercise.
Just remember the dotted quarter note = three 8th note in distance.
Good luck and go slow, dont forget to count out loud.

16TH NOTE VARATIONS EXPLAINED

We have learnt our 16th note rests and how they're applied to our 16th note combinations, but we also have a musical short hand in our 16th note varations that don't require rests. So this is where we need to add up our notes like a notational jigsaw puzzle.

1 +a 2 +a 3 +a 4 +a   8th note plus two 16th notes = a qtr note, no need for a rest.

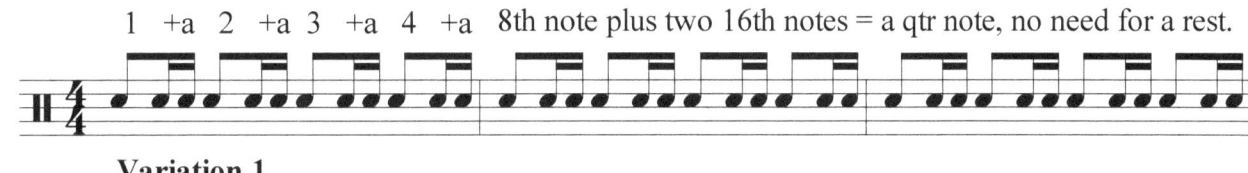

Variation 1

1e + 2e + 3e + 4e +   Reversed two 16th notes plus an 8th = a qtr note.

Variation 2

1 e a 2 e a 3 e a 4 e a   A 16th and a 8th a 16th still = a qtr note in value

Variation 3

Here we a 8th plus dot plus 16th = a qtr note.

1 a 2 a 3 a 4 a

Variation 4

Here we a 16th note rest, which still has value of a 16th, and three 16th notes to = the qtr.

e + a   e + a   e + a   e + a

Variation 5

1 e + 2 e + 3 e + 4 e +   Here we a 16th note rest plus a 16th note plus a 8th note = a qtr

Variation 6

1 e a 2 e a 3 e a 4 e a   And finally, a 16th note rest plus a 8th note plus a 16th note = a qtr

Variation 7

16TH NOTE VARIATION #1

Welcome to the first of your 16th note variations. Remember our mathematical jigsaw theory of notes and their values. Here we have one 8th note + two 16th notes = a qtr.
To count this variation it would be **2 +a**. Remember there's no need for rests in this equation.

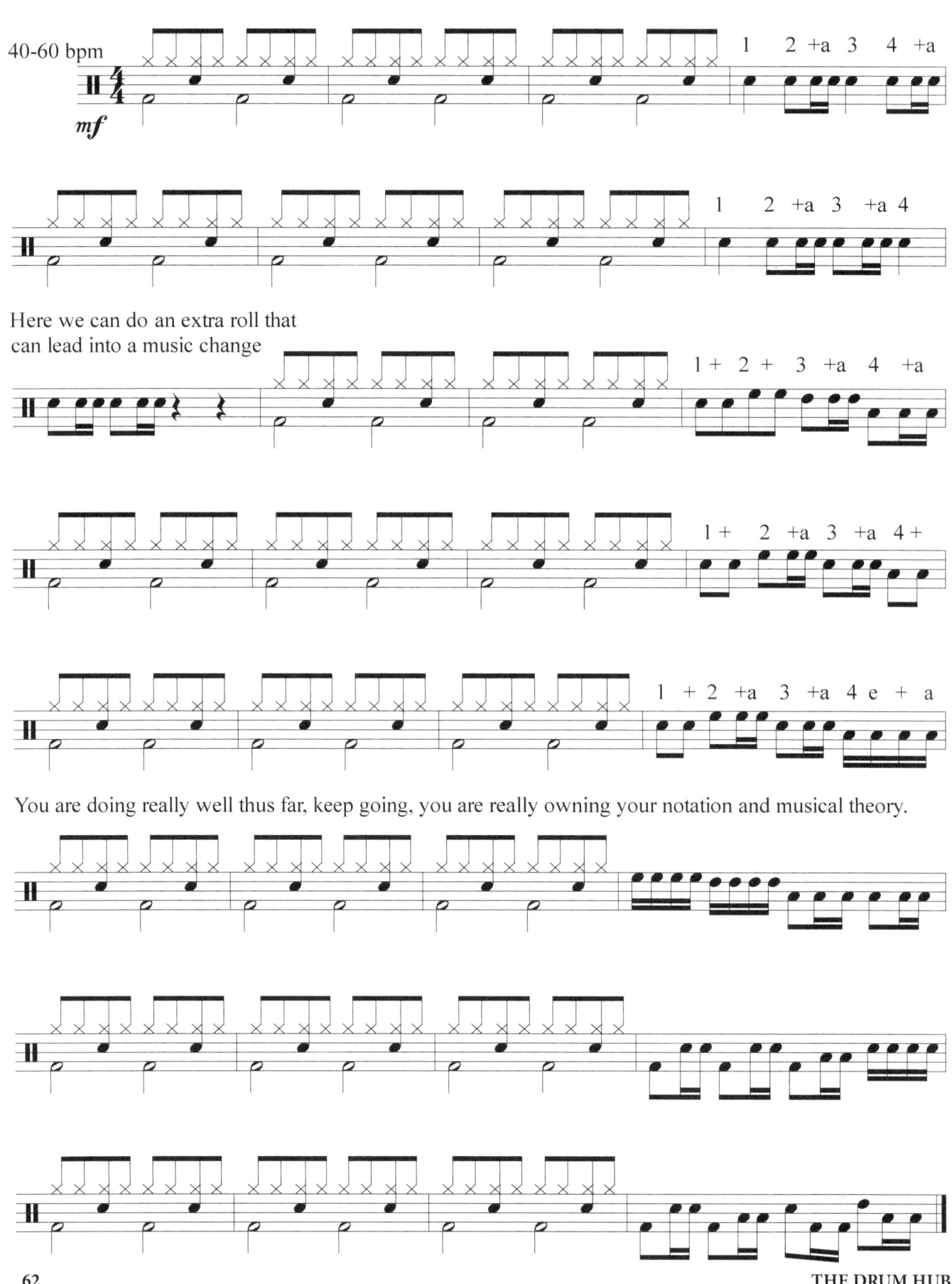

Here we can do an extra roll that
can lead into a music change

You are doing really well thus far, keep going, you are really owning your notation and musical theory.

16TH NOTE VARIATION #2

Ok lets try our variations without our rest now. Remember to count our notes and their values, two 16th's + one 8th = a qtr note. To count this variation it would be **2e+**
Take it slow and count your correct values.

Once again let try now without the help of the numbers. Take it slow count out loud.

THE DRUM HUB

16TH NOTE VARIATION #3

Just like the previous page lets do our mathematical jigsaw puzzle.
Remembering one 16th note + one 8th note + one 16th note = a qtr, to count this variation would be **1 e a**, there is no + in the equation.

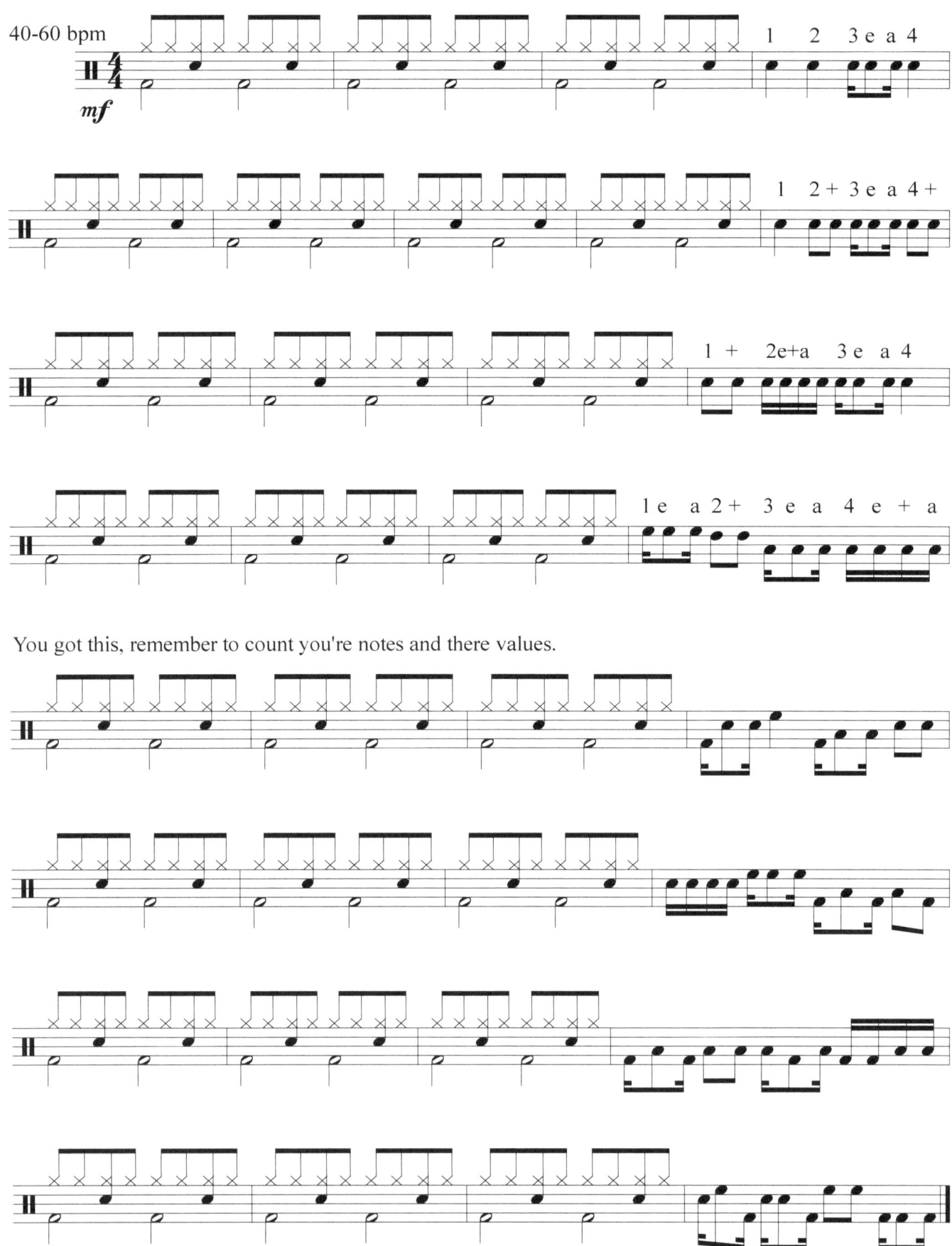

You got this, remember to count you're notes and there values.

16TH NOTE VARIATION #4

As you can see we are using the dotted note 16th variation, so remember the dot has a numeric value in this case it's a 16th. So we have a 8th note + a dot + one 16th adds up to the qtr, no need for rests.
To count this variation would be **1 a**

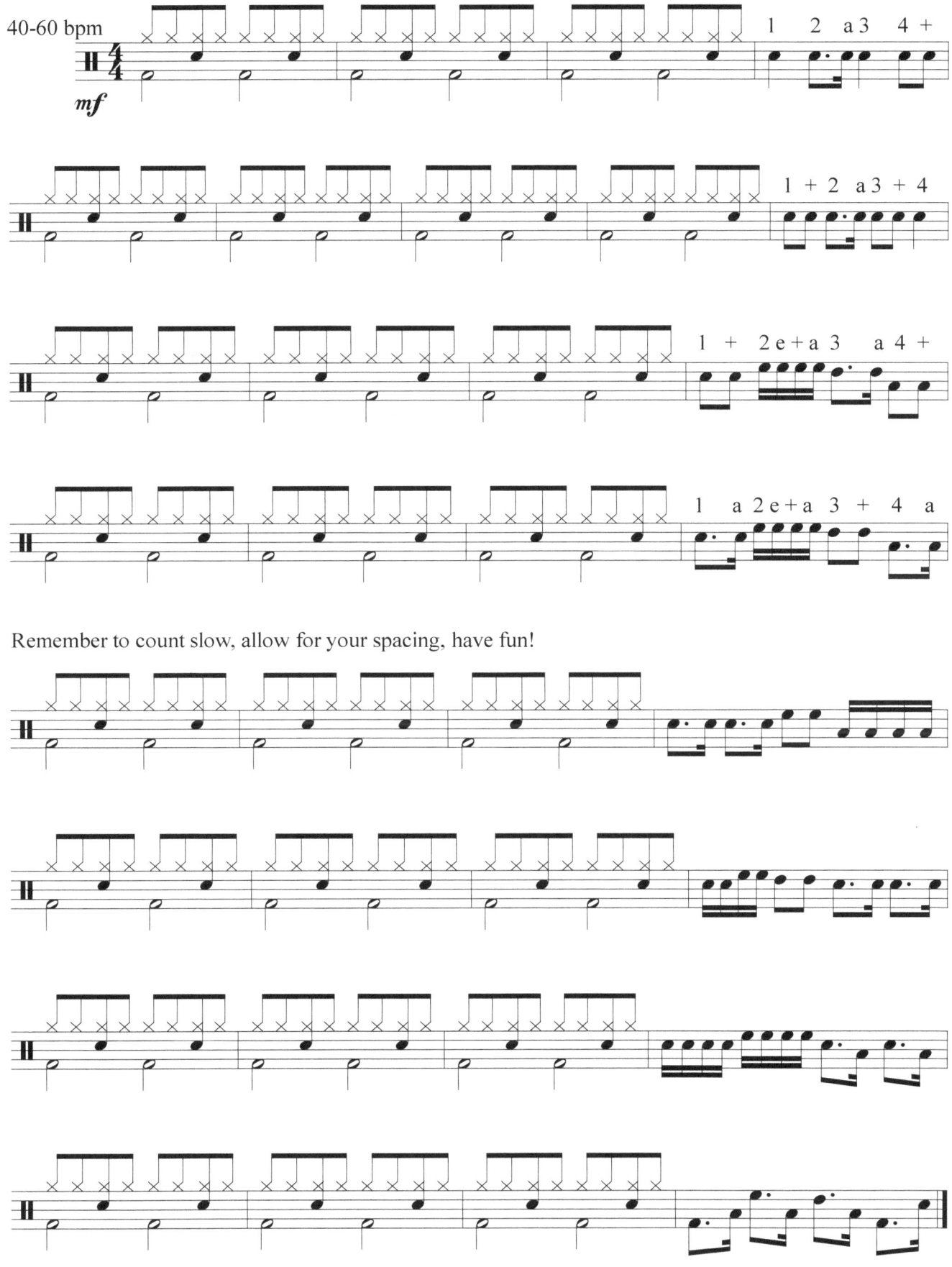

Remember to count slow, allow for your spacing, have fun!

THE DRUM HUB

16TH NOTE VARIATION #5

Variation #5 does require a 16th note rest at the start, reason being we are resting our primary number which is the 1 2 3 or even 4 count depending.
So here we have a 16th note rest + three 16th's, so in total it equals the qtr note.

Ok so now lets try our rhythms and rolls without the help of the numbers, good luck.

16TH NOTE VARIATION #6

Just like the previous variation, we too have a rest on our primary number.
So here we have a 16th note rest + a 16th note + a 8th note, in total it equals a whole qtr note
in value. To count this note would **e+**

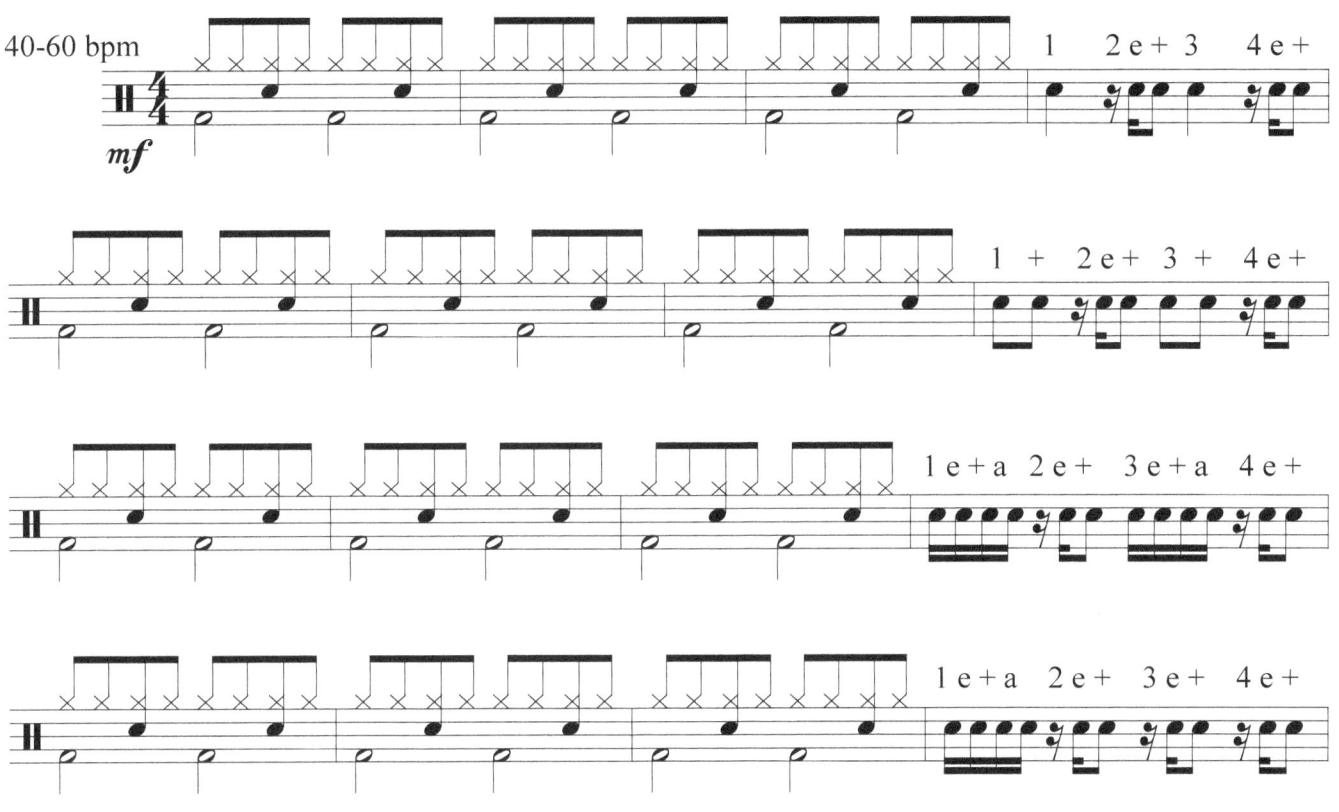

Ok getting a little harder now, remember to go slow and count out loud your variations.

THE DRUM HUB

16TH NOTE VARIATION #7

Ok welcome to our last 16th note variation, well done you have come so far with your notation and drum knowledge. As you can see we stil have a 16th note rest on the primary number.
So 16th note rest + 8th note + 16th note still adds up to equal our whole qtr note in value. To count this variation would be **e a**

Ok you're on your own now, remember to count slow and out loud. Good luck and have fun.

QUARTER NOTE WITH MIXED 16TH NOTE VARIATION

Ok so now a skill tester. We are going to apply all of our 16th note variations and qtr notes on snare, we're also going to introduce our left foot on the high hat chip.
Remember to go slow and count out loud. (What's our A,B,Cs) **A**lways **B**e **C**ounting

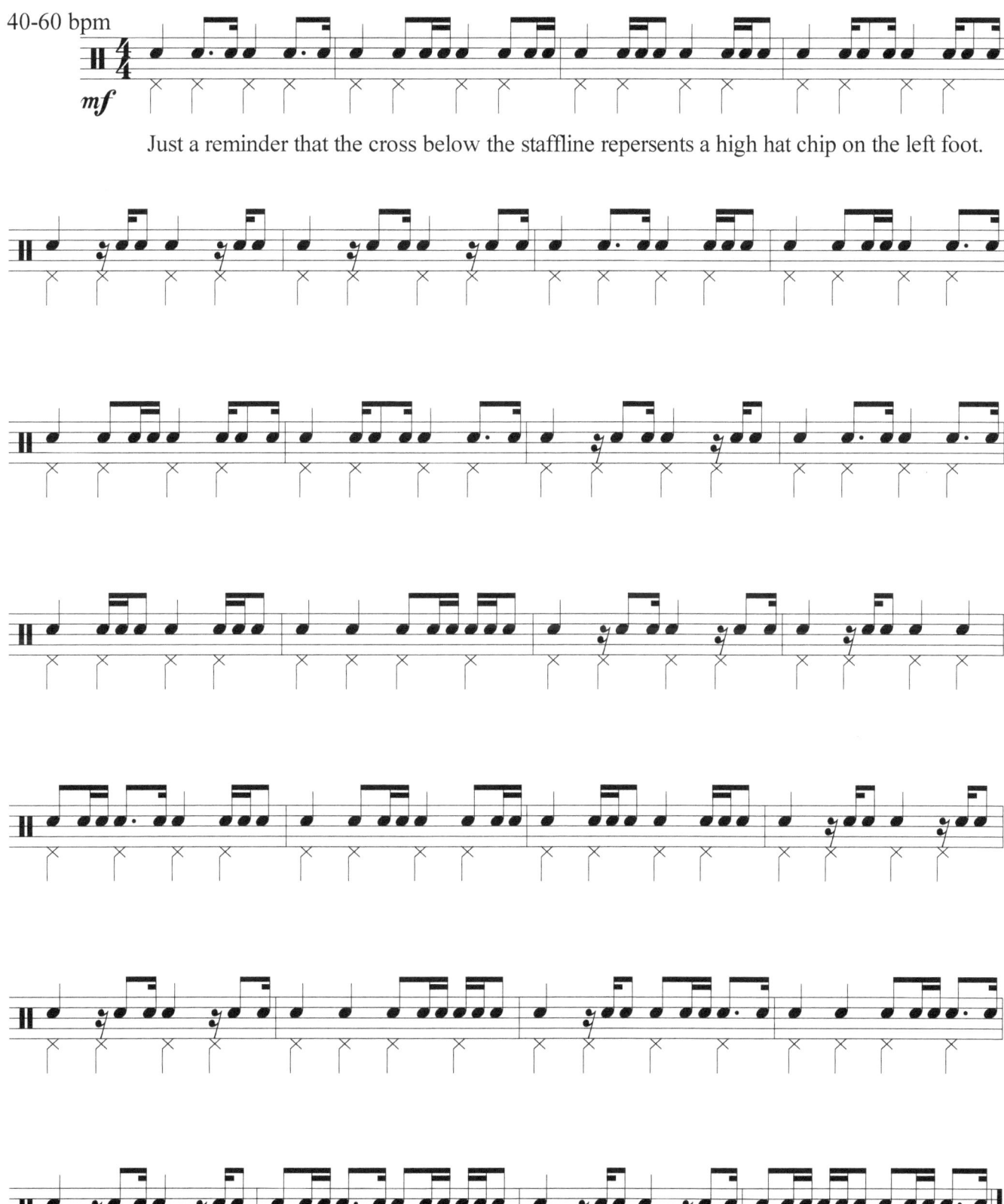

Just a reminder that the cross below the staffline repersents a high hat chip on the left foot.

THE DRUM HUB

8TH NOTE WITH MIXED 16TH NOTE VARIATION

Ok so just like the previous page were going to to try mix up our 8th notes now with all of your variations. Remember our left foot high hat to act as a metronome to keep us in time.

60-90 bpm

Remember the dotted repeat sign, play from the first two dots until you see the second two dots and repeat all the bars in between. In this case, there will be 8 bars in total.

16TH NOTES WITH 16TH VARIATIONS

Ok have fun with these guys, a lot more notes to contend with here. Go slow count out loud, these are a lot of fun when we pick up the tempo. Good luck!

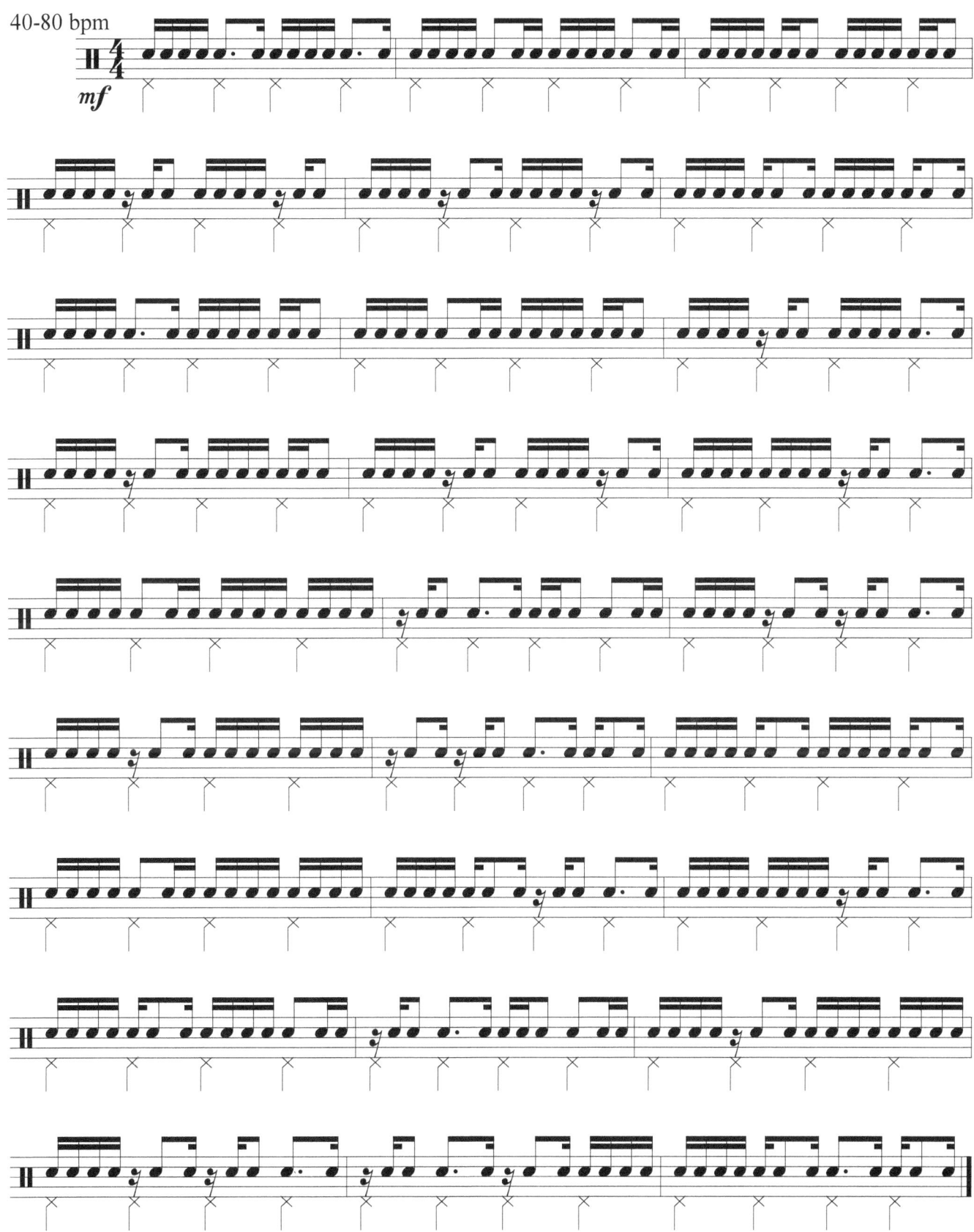

ALL 16TH NOTES VARIATIONS ON SNARE

Ok here's a challenge for you guys, lets try all variations on our snare drum, while keeping in time with our qtr note on the kick drum. This will be quite challenging, so take it slow, good luck!

MIXED RHYTHMS WITH VARIATIONS ON SNARE

Our objective here is to play the whole music score from top to bottom, go slow, we can always get faster as we develop our skill.

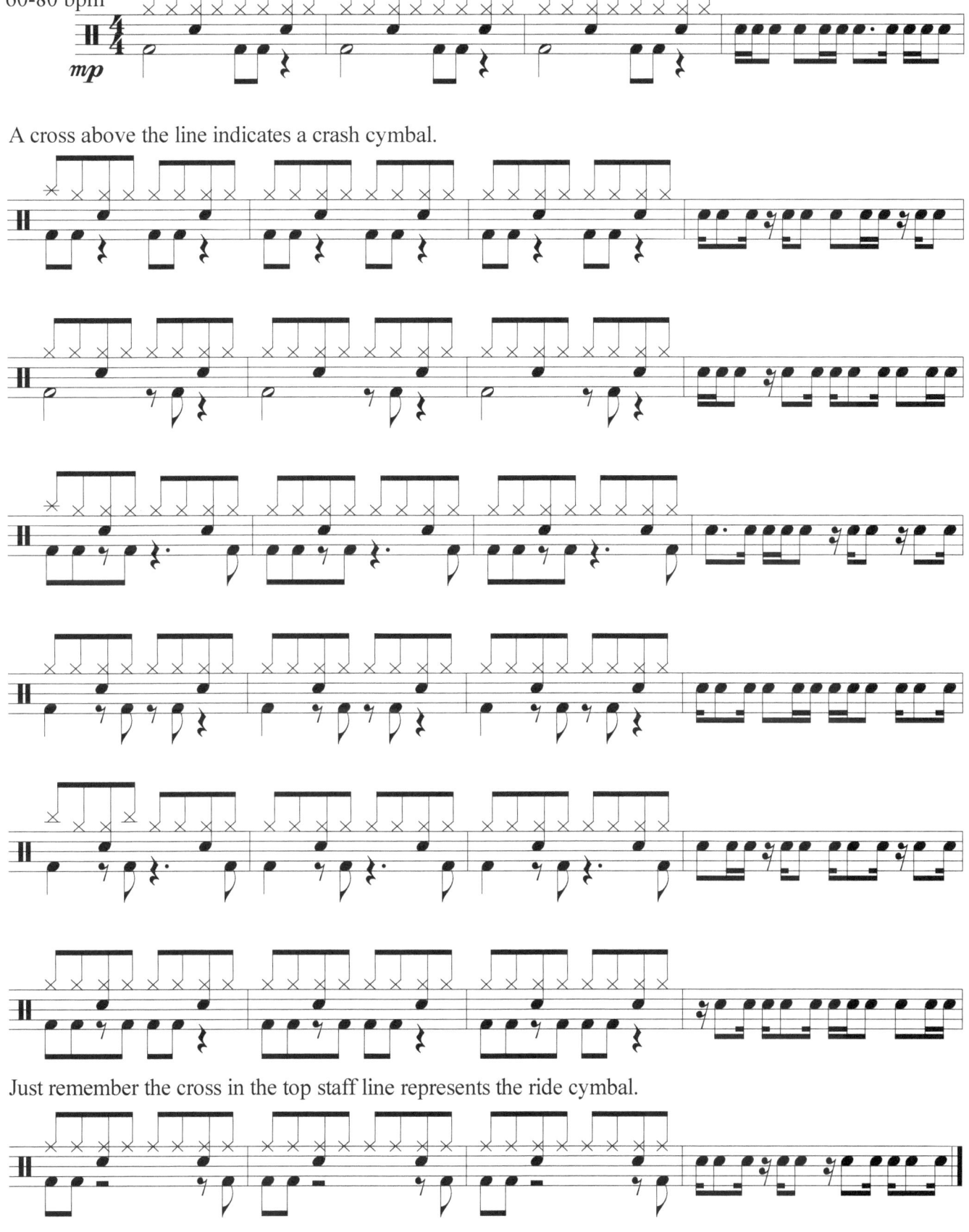

A cross above the line indicates a crash cymbal.

Just remember the cross in the top staff line represents the ride cymbal.

THE DRUM HUB

MIXED RHYTHMS WITH VARIATIONS ON TOMS

Rememeber guys to take note where our notes are sitting on the staff lines, remembering that each line represents a different drum. Refer to staff lines and meanings in front of book.

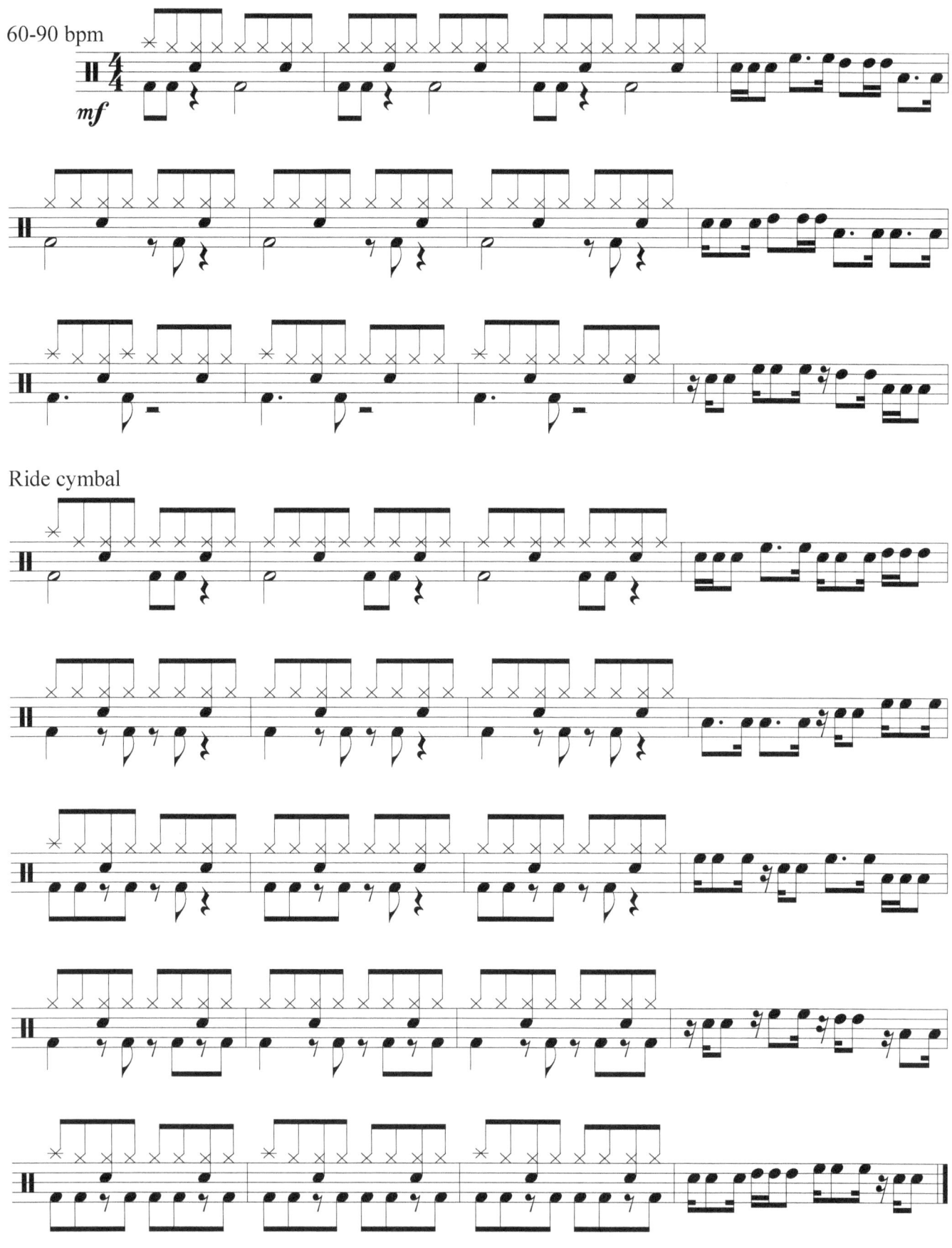

QUARTER 8THS 16TH NOTE VARIATIONS COMBINATION STUDY

QUARTER 8THS 16TH NOTE VARIATIONS WITH RESTS

Ok guys well done, you have retained so much musicial notation thus far, excellent job! We now have our variations with our mixed note rests, take your time and remember to allow for the spacing of your rests.

16TH NOTE RHYTHMS WITH VARIATIONS

Here we have our 16th note rhythm patterns with all 7 variations on our kick drum. Go slow and remember to count your 16th notes on your high hat. Good luck and have fun on this new style of playing.

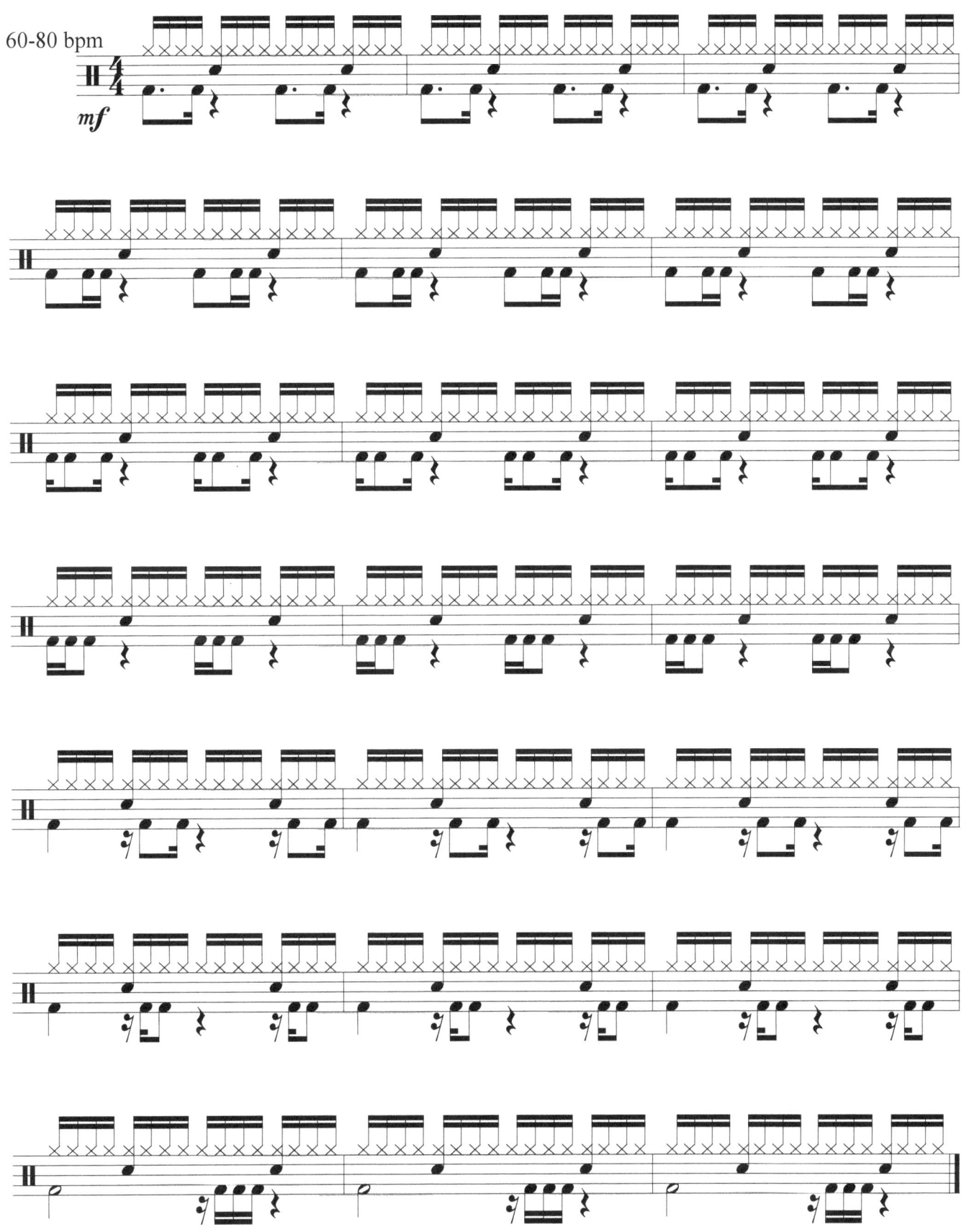

16TH NOTE RHYTHMS WITH MIXED VARIATIONS

Just like the previous page, we now have our mixed variations on our kick drum, these are a lot of fun, so go slow and enjoy these harder rhythms. Good luck.

40-60 bpm

16TH NOTE VARIATIONS WITH SNARE ROLLS

Ok guys there is a lot of information and difficult notation on this rhythm and roll exercise. Take it slow and do the best you can. Remember we can always speed up the tempo as we get more fluent in reading this drum score.

16TH NOTE VARIATIONS WITH TOM ROLLS

Remember guys we are getting some real complex tom rolls here, go slow and count out your 16th note variations. You're doing a great job learning your notation thus far, keep up the great work.

8TH & 16TH SEPERATION EXCERISES

Just like in our earlier seperation exercises, we had qtrs over 8th's. Now we have 8th's over 16th's. A lot of these hand foot coordination excercises, will give you a feel of the motion. The hand comes up the foot goes down, bit like an opposite up down effect.

We are going to eliminate the snare in this exercise, so we can focus on the seperation side of things. Good luck and do the best you can.

8TH & 16TH NOTE RHYTHM TRANSITIONS

Once again we have our rhythm transitons going from 8th notes to 16th notes on our high hat. Remember to keep the same tempo throughout to get that nice cut time feel, Go slow to start with, these can get quite difficult. Remember to count out loud.

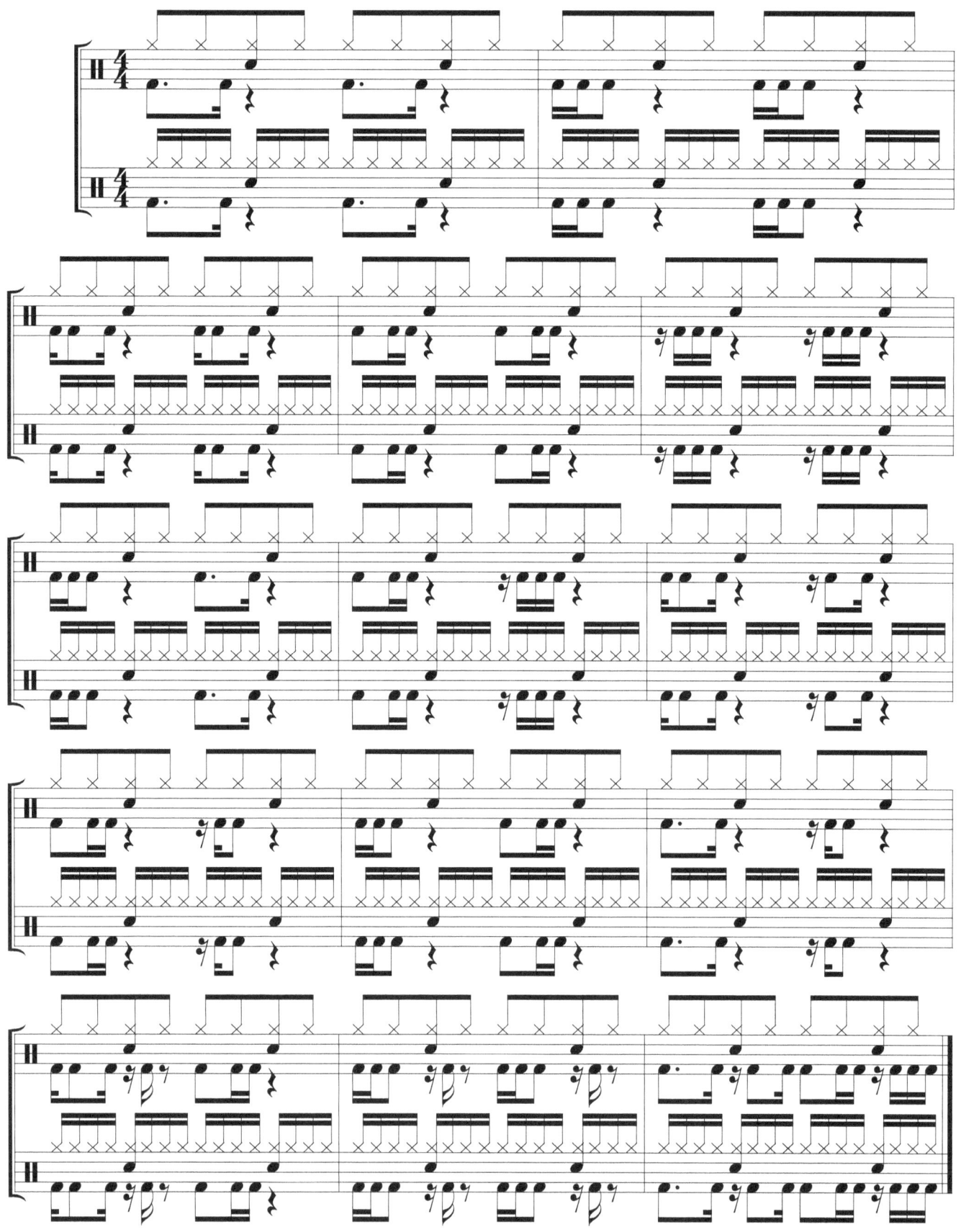

MIXED NOTES AND VARAIATION RHYTHMS PATTERNS

Good luck with these rhythm patterns, these are getting up there now, remember to focus on your separation exercises. That opposite feel up and down motion, you are doing so well. These are very fun but complex rhythms you are playing now, excellent job!

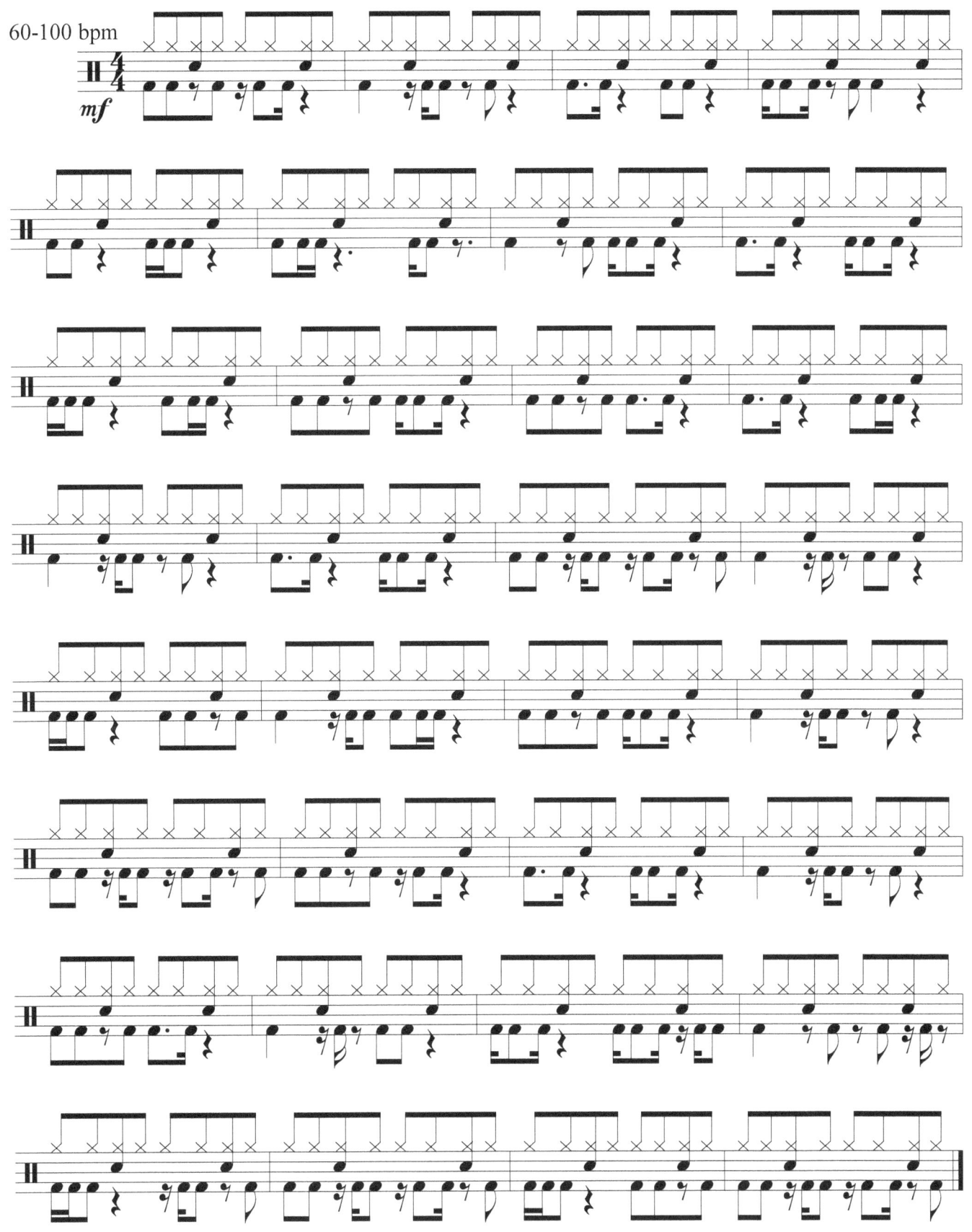

8THS OVER 16TH RYHTHM PATTERNS

Just like the previous page, we're going to focus on our separation techniques, but with variations only this time. Still it will be quite tricky so go slow, count out loud and have fun.

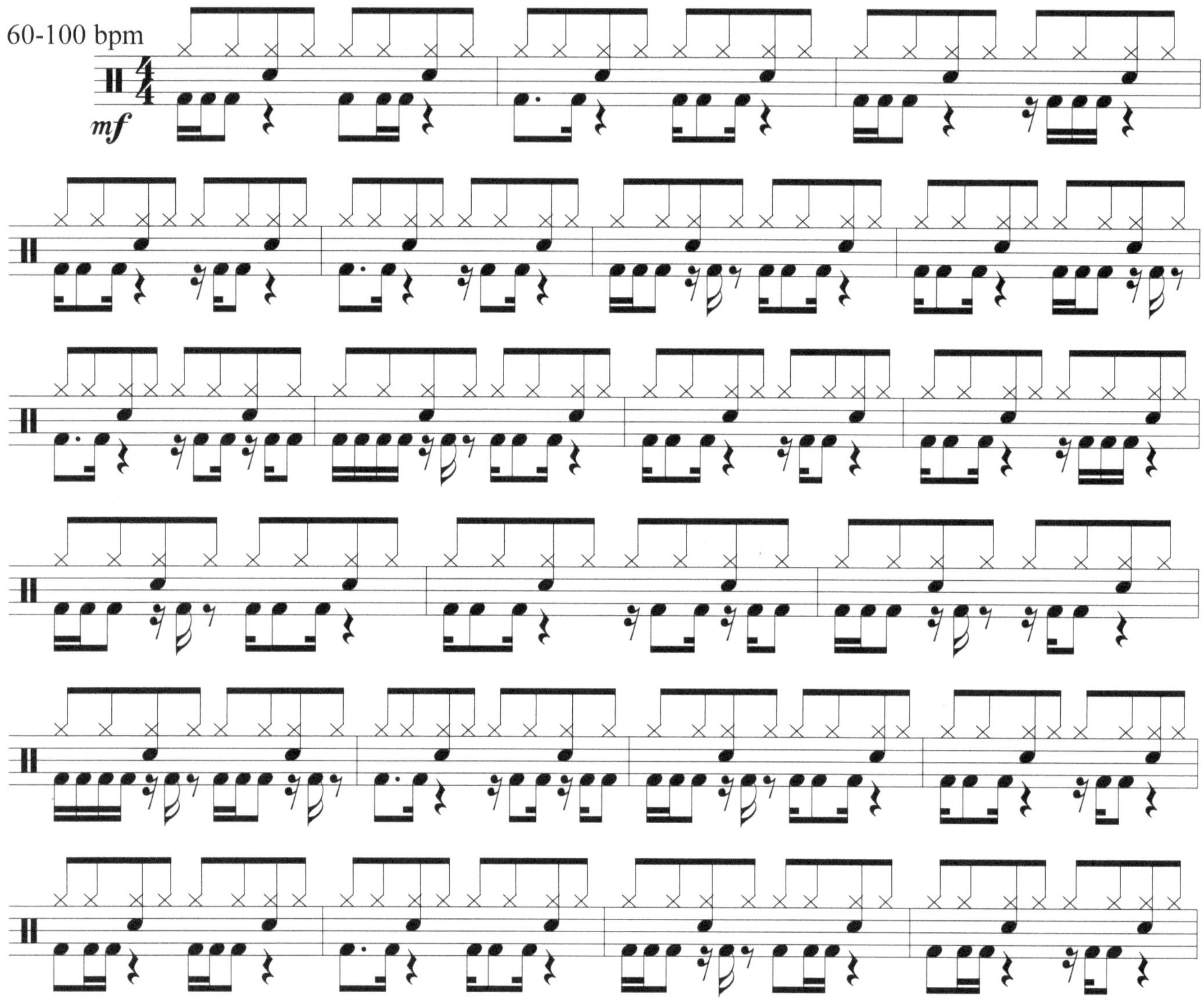

60-100 bpm

Notice where the cross is on the staffline, now lets try it with our open hand posture on our ride cymbal

MIXED NOTE SNARE DISPLACEMENTS

In this exercise we are going to focus on adding more snares to our rhythm playing. Thus we get more of a funk style to our playing. These are very fun rhythms to play, enjoy go slow and have fun.

60-90 bpm

Ok lets start off easy, remembering to count out loud.

8TH OVER 16TH RHYTHM AND SNARE DISPLACEMENTS

Ok guys were really going to start to ramp up our complex rhythms now. We will be using our 16th note variations on our feet, as well as our high hat and snare displacements.
Go slow these are quite tricky, remembering our ABC's process.

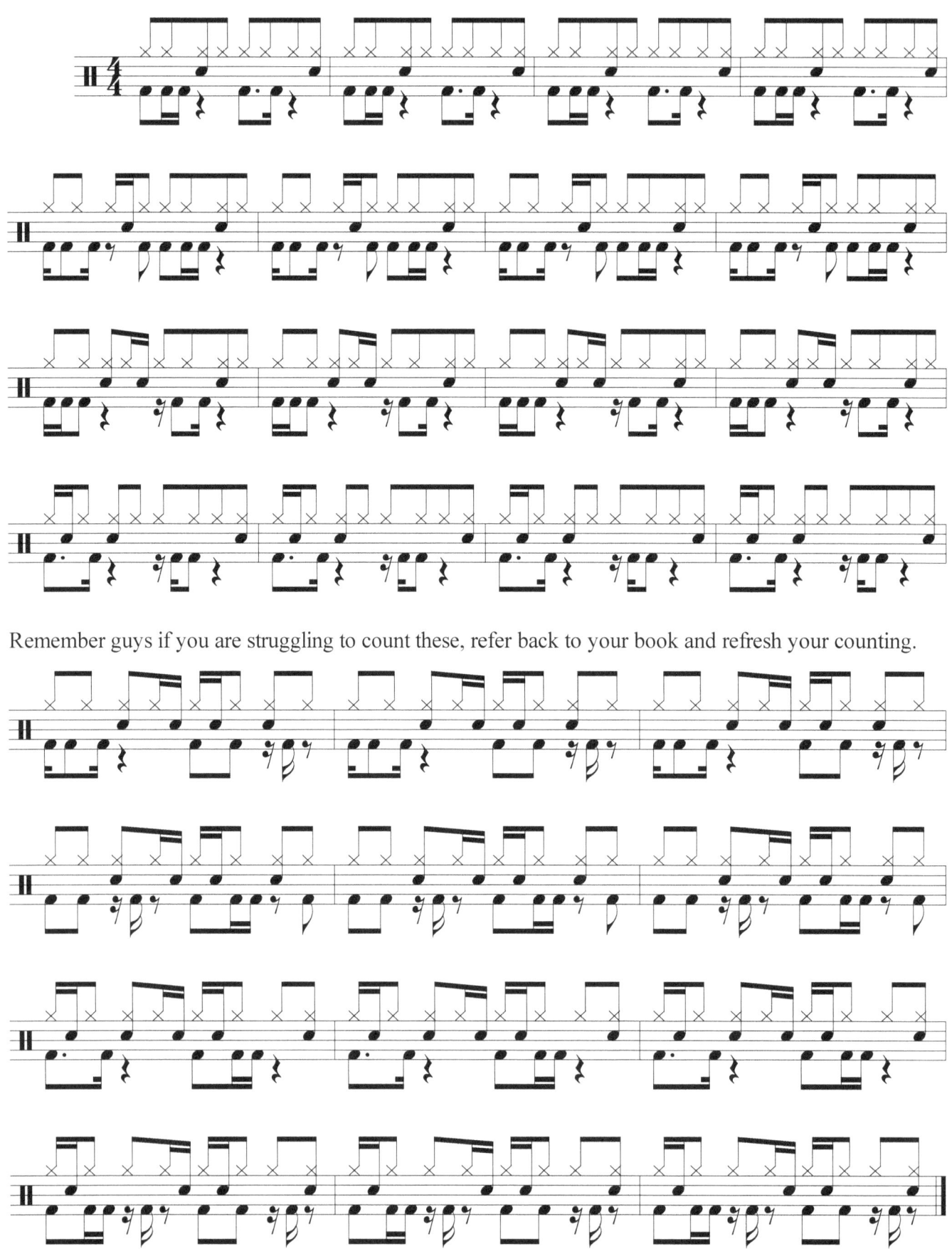

Remember guys if you are struggling to count these, refer back to your book and refresh your counting.

MIXED HIGH HAT RHYTHMS #1

Ok guys, something a little different here. We're going to keep it easy on the kick drum, whilst mixing up some complex rhythm patterns on the high hat.

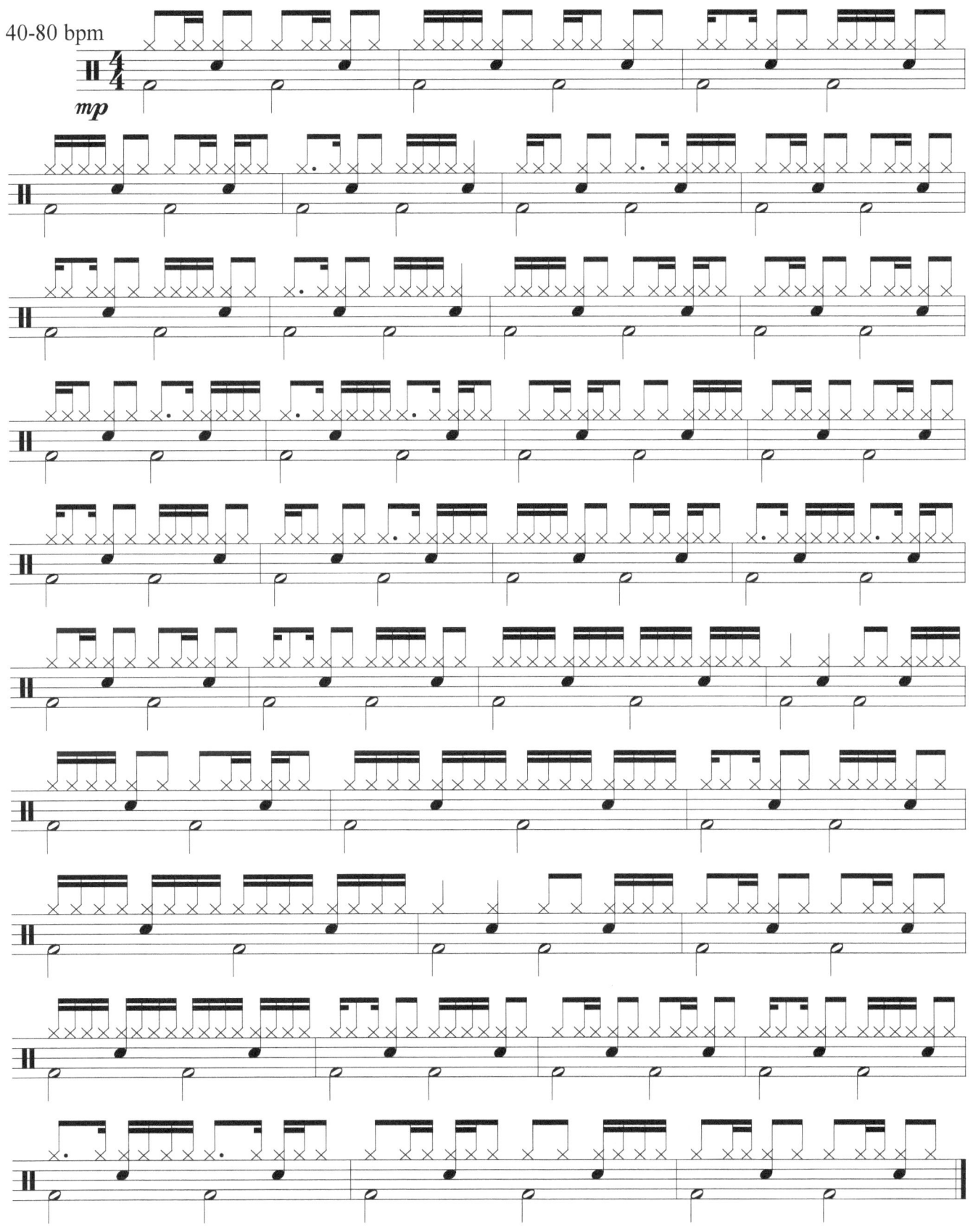

MIXED HIGH HAT RHYTHMS #2

Ok guys like the previous page, these high hat rhythm patterns are getting very tricky. Go super slow and count out your variations on the high hat, our kick drum will be very challenging as well, good luck!

SOLO EXERCISE

Ok guys our solos are getting a little more complex now with our bigger notes and variations. Remember all our repeat signs and 1st and 2nd endings. Go slow and refer to the front of the book for our tempo marks and dynamics and D.S al Fine. Good luck.

STUDENT PRACTICAL SUMMARY

On these blank staff lines use your bars to practise writing down the notation that you have learnt thus far. Try adding in your rests and write out some of your favourite rhythms. Enjoy the process.

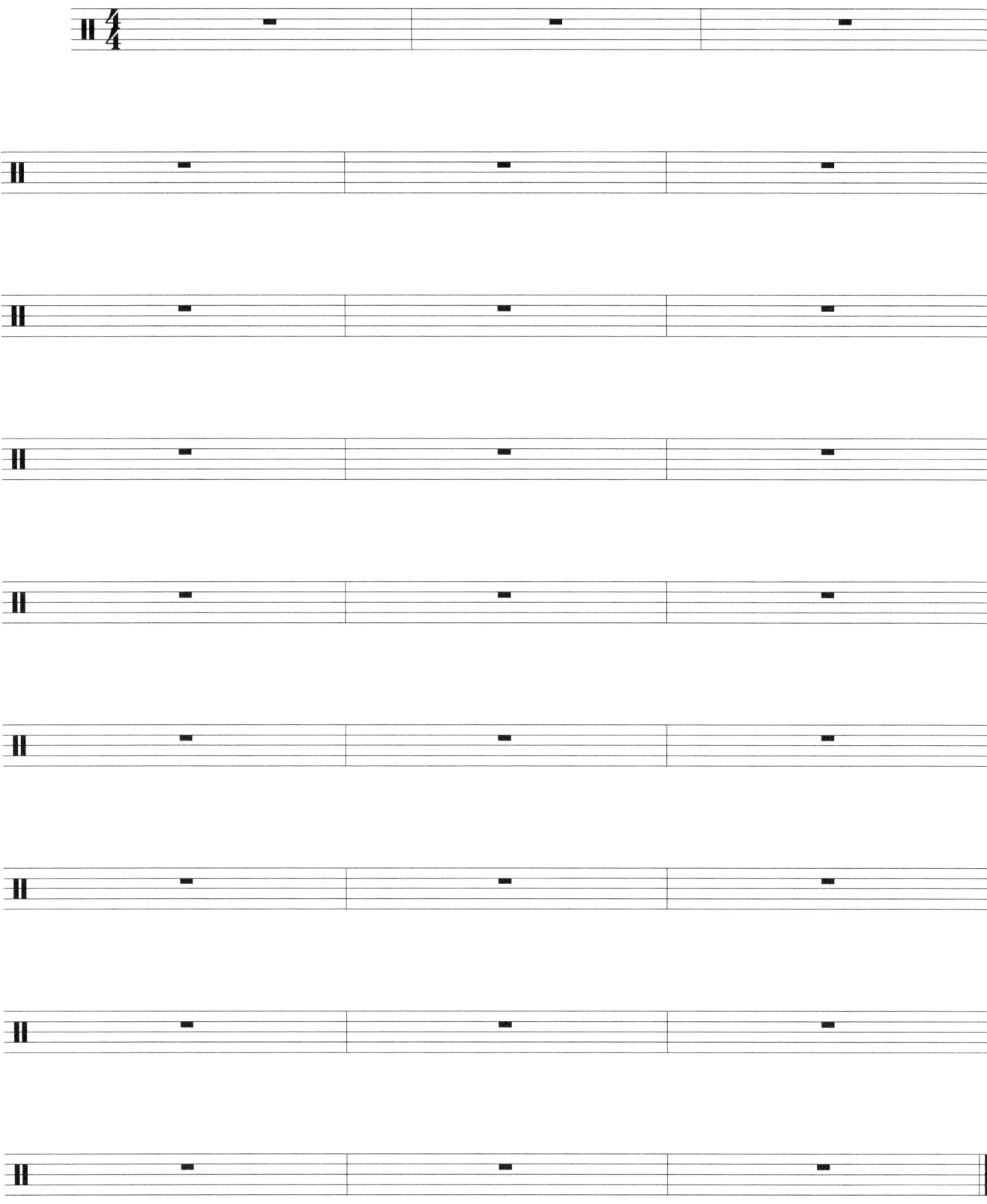

TIME SIGNATURES AND COUNTING

Ok guys when it come to time signatures, there's a few things to remember. We have three types of time signatures, there's common time 2\4, 3/4 and 4\4, there's are also odd time signatures of 5\4, 6\4, 7\4, etc. And lastly, there are compound time signatures 3\8, 6\8, 9\8, 12\8. Just remember that the top number is how many beats in a bar and the bottom number is the type of note we are using.

Rhythmic values:
An eighth note (♪) = 1/2 beat
A quarter note (♩) = 1 beat
A half note (𝅗𝅥) = 2 beats
A dotted half note (𝅗𝅥.) = 3 beats
A whole note (𝅘) = 4 beats

Pay attention to the time signature being used in each exercise.

ODD TIME SIGNATURES

Welcome to odd time signatures guys. These measures consist of adding more than just the 4/4 beat. There's no rules when it comes to time signatures, all we are doing is adding extra beats to extend the length of our bar. Time changes are a very different way of playing our rhythms. Enjoy and have fun with these.

COMPOUND TIME SIGNATURES

Welcome guys to your compound time signatures, what we have here is the dotted qtr note pulse on the foot. Dotted qtr note = three 8th notes, hence our rhythmic pattern on our high hat.

Ok guys lets try playing some random compound time rhythms, go slow and get use to the timming, enjoy.

THE DRUM HUB

Chapter 5

TRIPLETS EXPLAINED

Welcome to triplets explained. Throughout the whole book we have focused on all notes being cut and doubled, qtr to 8ths, 8th's to 16th's ect. Well, the triplet note is a irregular note, we want to be able to squeeze 3 8th's notes into the space of one qtr note. Lets just say hypothectical qtr = 10 but 3x3= 9 right? Just like 3 8th note doesn't add up into 10, so we have to stretch our notes to last the distance of a qtr note.

See how we are fitting 3 8ths note into the count of 1 qtr

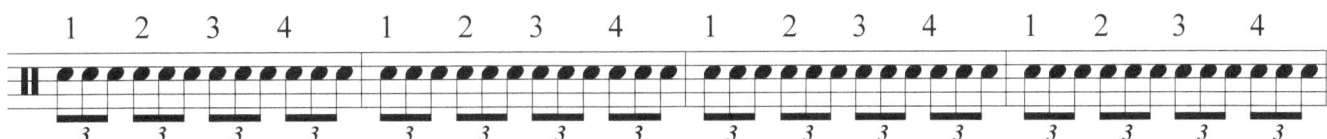

How we want to count the full 8th note triplet is.

1-Trip-Let **2**-Trip-Let **3**-Trip-Let **4**-Trip-Let

How to count the abbreviated triplet note.

THE DRUM HUB

QUARTER NOTE WITH TRIPLETS

Ok guys, now that you have mastered the triplet count on the previous page, we are now mixing our qtr and triplets notes together. You will feel like a slight delay in your playing like a dragged out note feel, this is normal because you are internally stretching the irregular triplet note out.

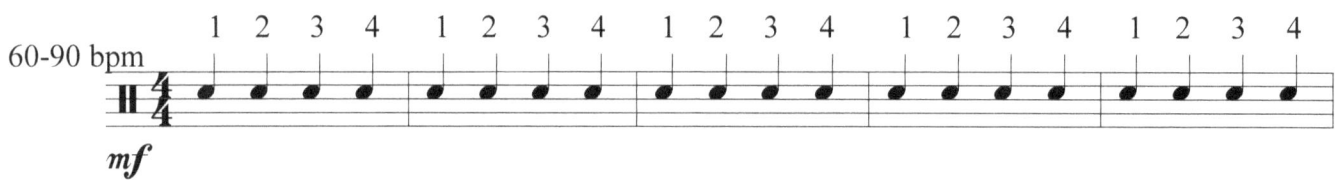

Ok guys lets try without the help of the numbers, also adding foot on the kick, you got this!

8TH NOTES WITH TRIPLETS

Ok guys just like the last page, remember to count out those stretched 8th note triplets.
Count out loud and take it slow.

Ok lets try some random snare exercises with our added foot on the kick drum. Have fun!

16TH NOTES WITH TRIPLETS

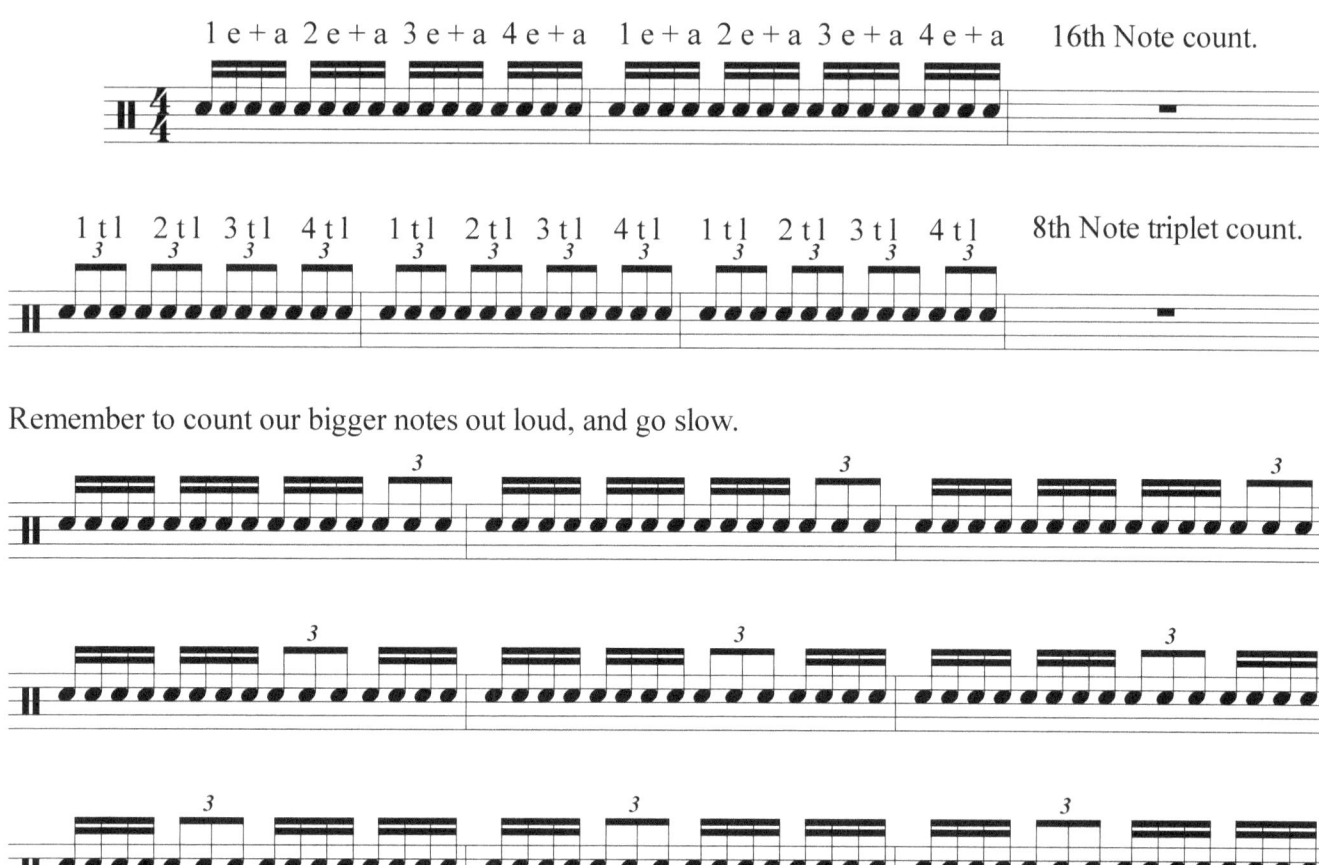

Remember to count our bigger notes out loud, and go slow.

Ok guys once again, lets add our kick drum in on the qtr note acting as our metronome

QUARTER 8THS 16THS NOTES WITH TRIPLETS

Ok guys, we are starting to have fun with these triplets now, enjoy your mixed notes and have fun with these exercises. Go slow, we can always speed up our tempo at a later date.

60-100 bpm

8TH NOTE TRIPLET ACCENTS

Remember guys, our accents signs above the corresponding note is played louder than the other notes. Try and keep the non accented notes really light, as if they were ghost notes.

8TH NOTE TRIPLET REST

Ok guys, now we're dealing with the 8th note triplet rest, one thing to keep in mind is that the 8th note rest itself applies exactly that same as in would in a regular 8th note as to an irregular note. Simply it's still just a 8th note rest in value.

MIXED NOTE AND REST EXERCISE

Just like the previous page guys, we are dealing with a lot of rests and their values. We are adding in the left foot high hat chip this time. Remember to count slowly and be mindful of the duration and length of our rests and the distance they last for. Have fun!

8TH NOTE TRIPLET RHYTHMS

Welcome guys to the brand new triplet rhythm page. Remember to count your triplets on the high hat and slowly add in your kick drum. You will get a nice swing type feel on your rhythm sections.

8TH NOTE TRIPLET RHYTHMS WITH ROLLS

Ok guys these are a lot of fun. We are doing our standard 8th note rhythms with our irregular rolls around the kit. These rhythms and rolls will feel a little peculiar, reason being mixing our straight mathematical 4/4 rhythms with the triplet irregular rolls. You will still feel that swing motion with your rolls around the kit. Good luck.

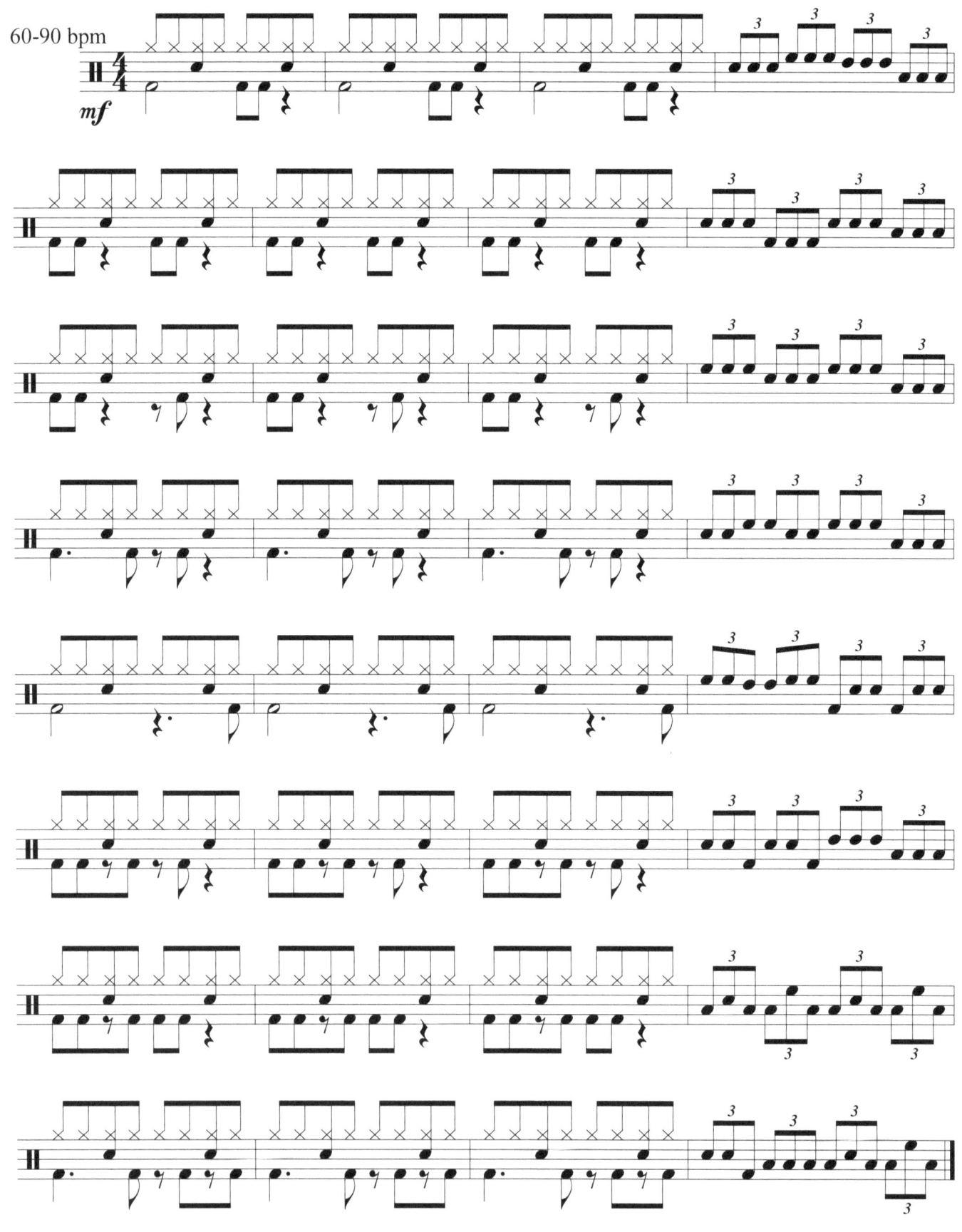

8TH NOTE MATHEMATICAL RHYTHMS WITH IRREGULAR TRIPLETS

Ok guys these are a lot of fun. We are doing our standard 8th note rhythms with our irregular rolls around the kit. These rhythms and rolls will feel a little peculiar, reason being mixing our straight mathematical 4/4 rhythms with the triplet irregular rolls. You will still feel that swing motion with your rolls around the kit. Good luck.

8TH NOTE VARIATION RHYTHMS WITH WITH IRREGULAR TRIPLETS

Getting a little harder now guys, remember your 8th's over 16th's separation exercises, start slow and get those irregular triplets in. Good luck!

SOLO EXERCISE

We have a really advanced music score here guys, remember to allow for all your rests, and make sure we stretch those 8th note triplets out in our timmimg. Remember to refer to the front of your book to see dynamics and tempo marks and D.C al coda. Enjoy guys

STUDENT PRACTICAL SUMMARY

On these blank staff lines use your bars to practise writing down the notation that you have learnt thus far. Try adding in your rests and write out some of your favourite rhythms. Have Fun.

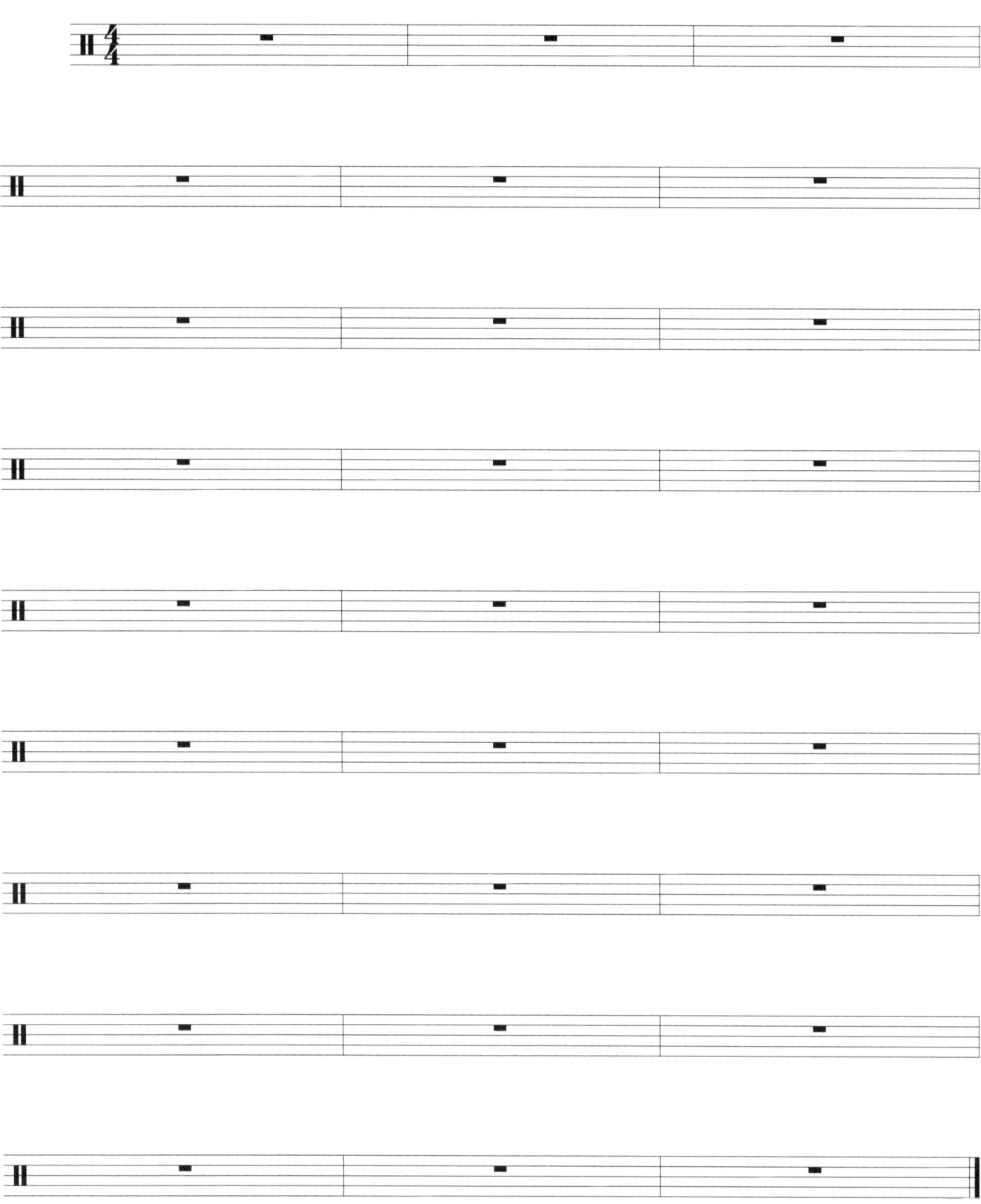

Chapter 6

16TH NOTE TRIPLET EXPLAINED

Ok guys, welcome to the 16th note triplet. Just like previous discussions about irregular 8th note triplets, they squeeze into the qtr note. We now have three 16th note triplets squeezing into one 8th note, hence doubling our count from **1 t l 2 t l 3 t l 4 t l** to our brand new count of **1tl+tl 2tl+tl 3tl+tl 4tl+tl**

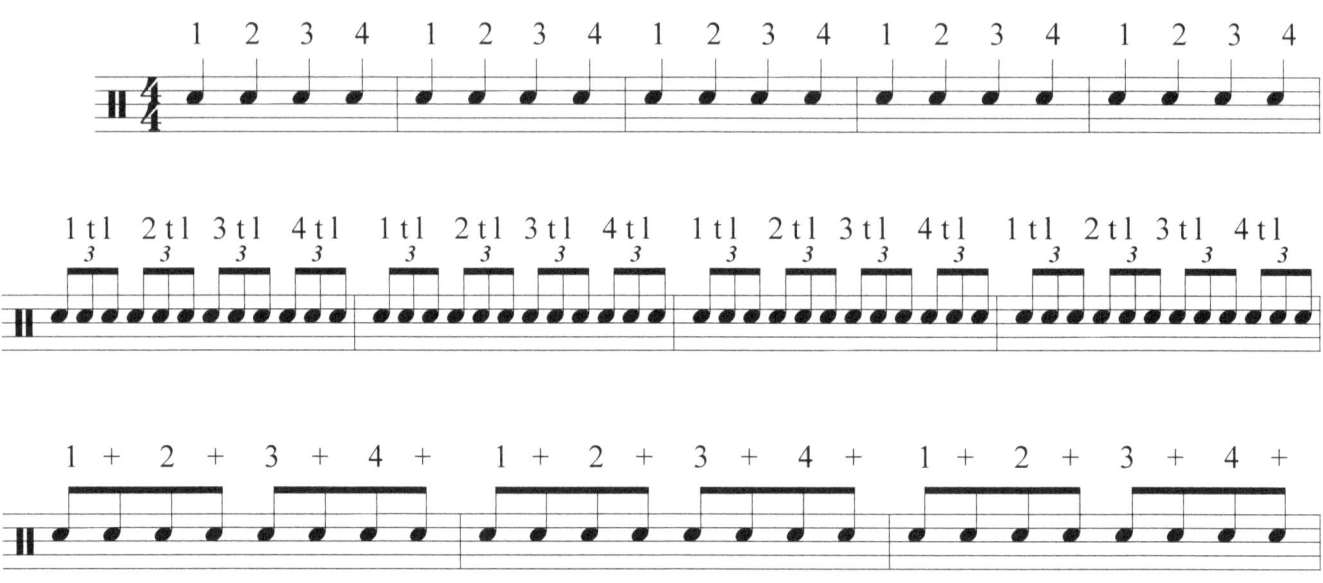

And how to pronounce this brand new count is

1 trip-let and trip-let   2 trip-let and trip-let   3 trip-let and trip-let   4 trip-let and trip-let

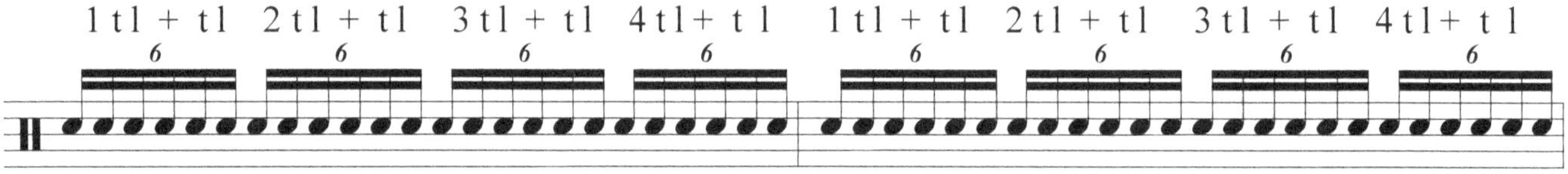

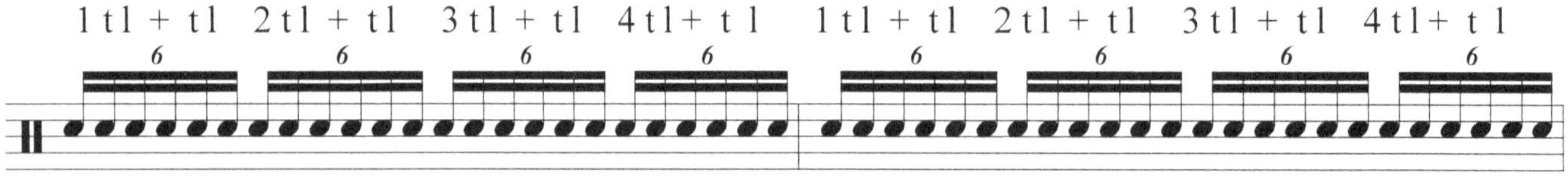

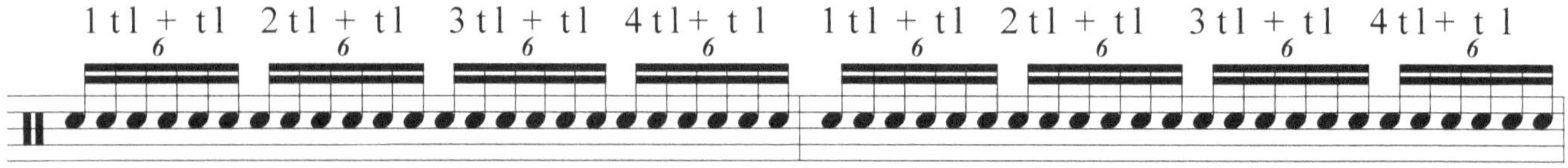

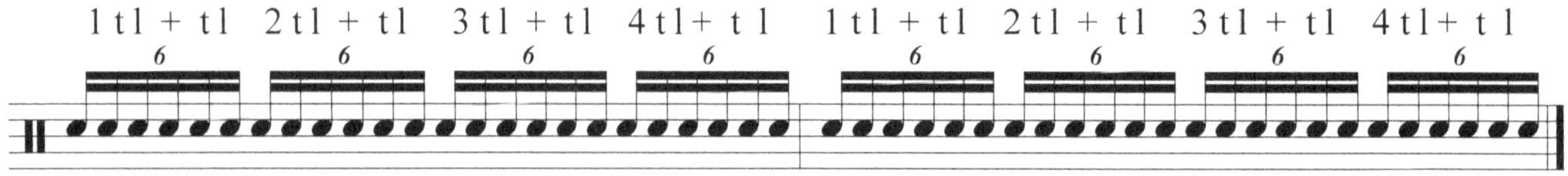

QUARTER NOTE WITH 16TH NOTE TRIPLETS

Well done understanding the 16th note triplet, we now have our qtr and 16th note triplet exercise. Remember to go slow and really stretch those triplets out. Were starting to explore our bigger notes now, well done. Also remember our A,B,C's. (always be counting).

40-60 bpm

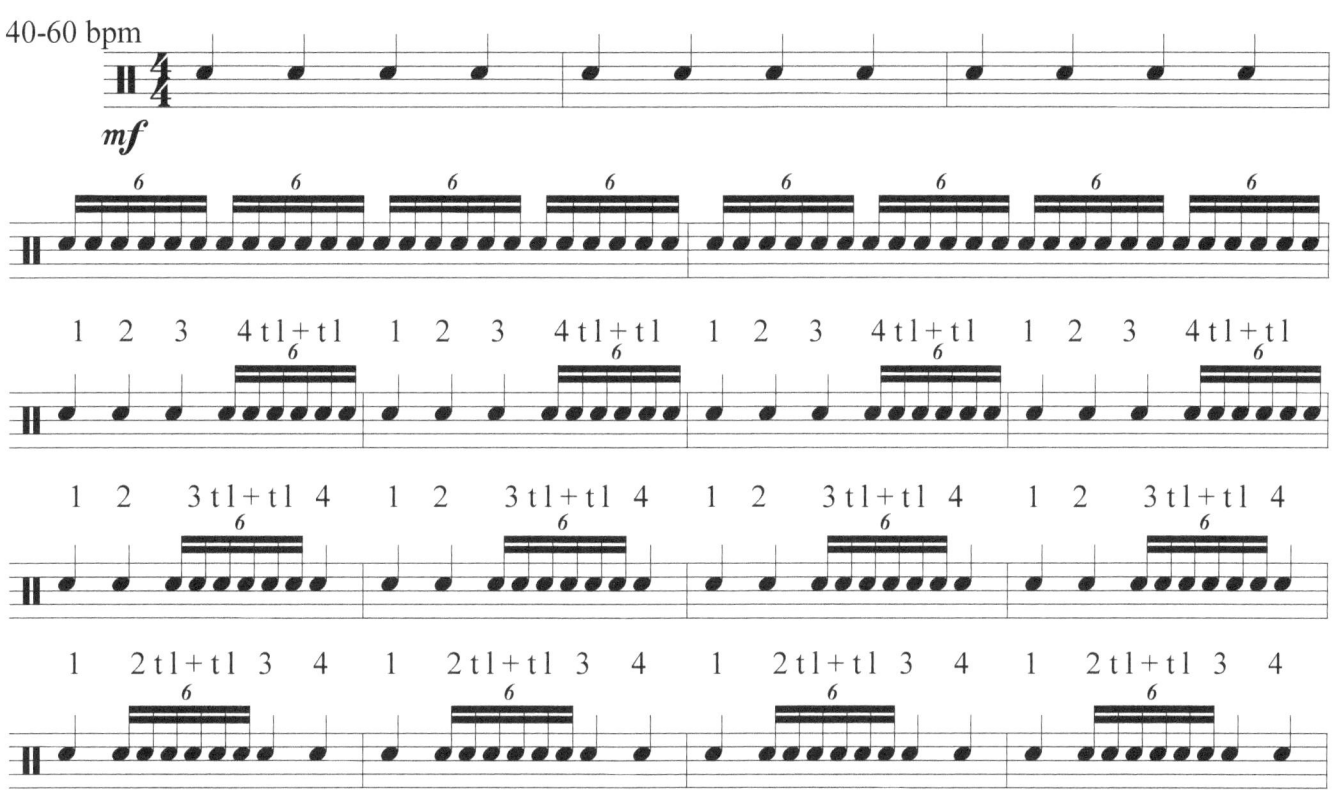

Ok guys lets try count our 16th note triplets without the help of the numbers. Enjoy try your best.

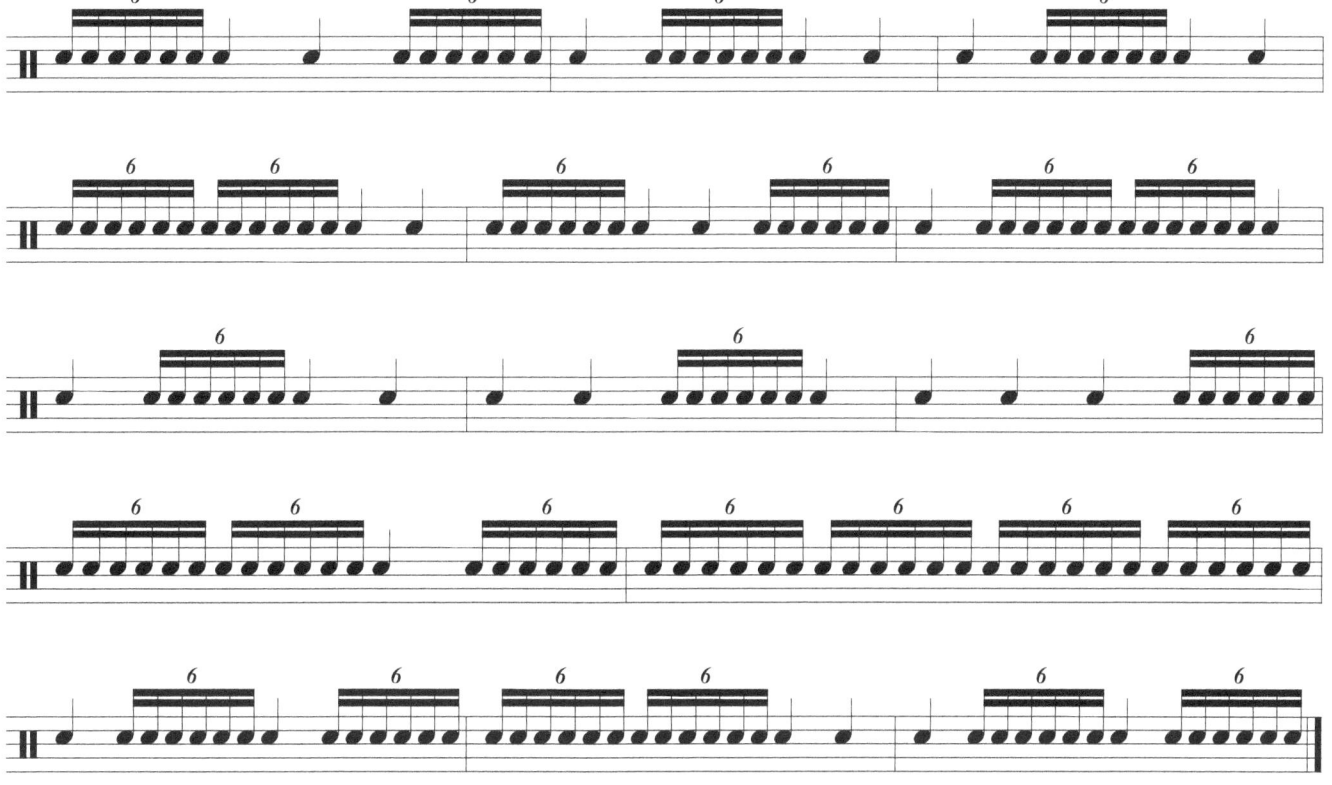

THE DRUM HUB

8TH NOTE WITH 16TH NOTE TRIPLETS

Just like the previous page, remember to allow for our correct spacing for our notes, and get those 16th note triplets stretched out lasting the same distance as the 8th note.

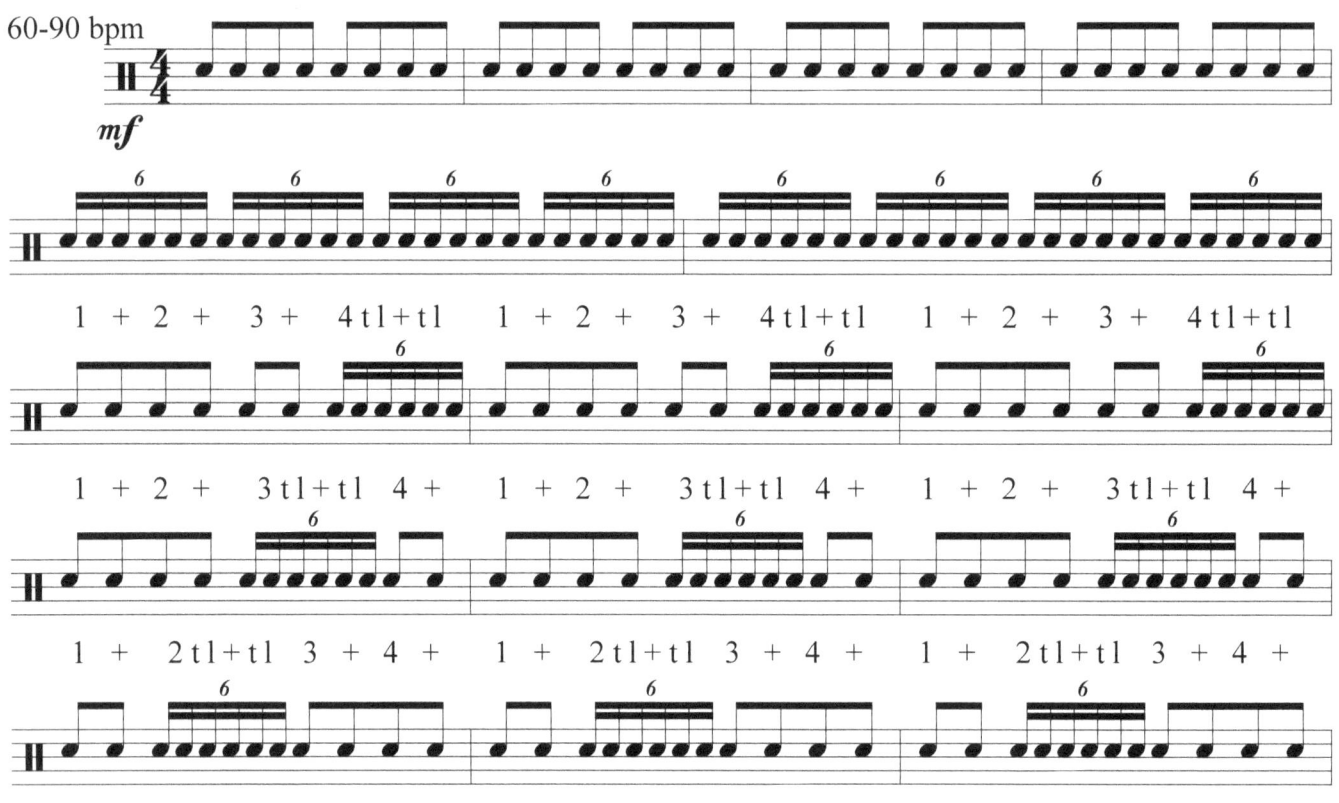

Ok once again guys lets try counting our 8th and 16th note triplets, without the help of the numbers.

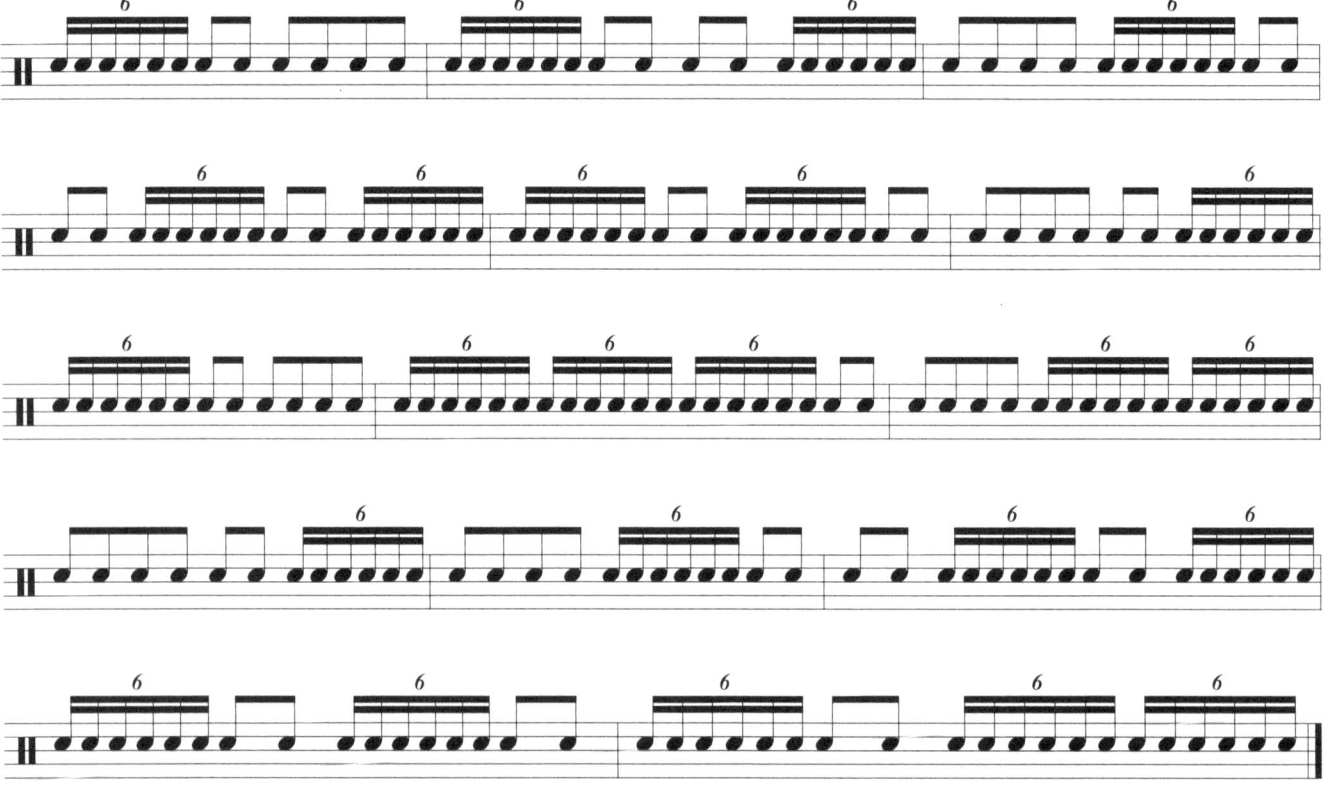

16TH NOTE WITH 16TH NOTE TRIPLETS

We are starting to get into our bigger note realm now, remember to count your 16th notes and your irregular triplets out loud. Enjoy.

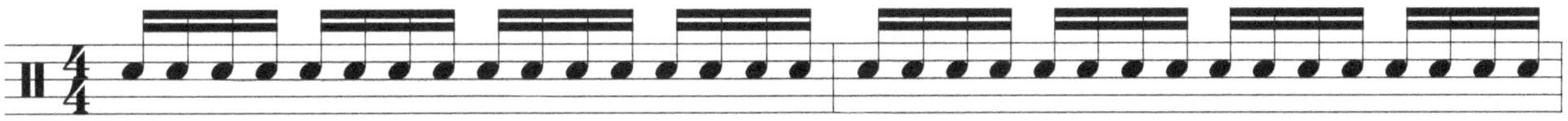

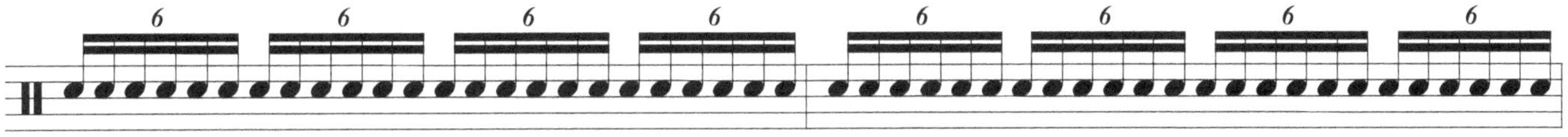

1 e + a   2 e + a   3 e + a   4 t l + t l   1 e + a   2 e + a   3 e + a   4 t l + t l

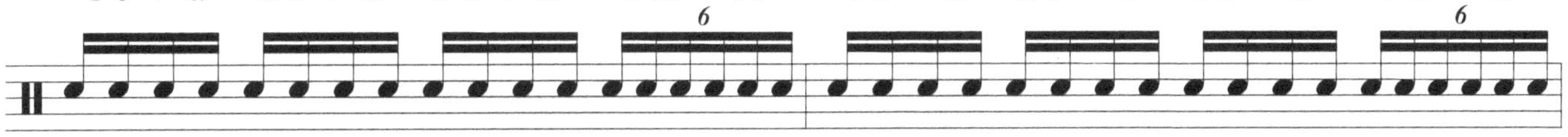

1 e + a   2 e + a   3 t l + t l   4 e + a   1 e + a   2 e + a   3 t l + t l   4 e + a

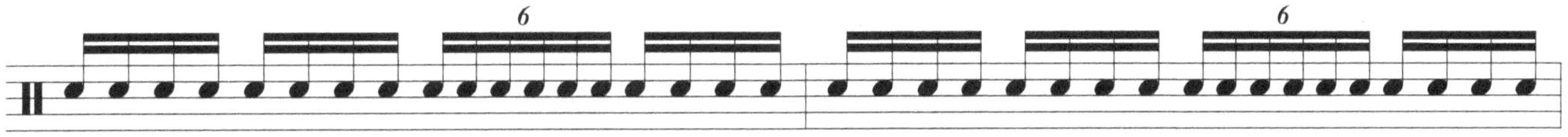

1 e + a   2 t l + t l   3 e + a   4 e + a   1 e + a   2 t l + t l   3 e + a   4 e + a

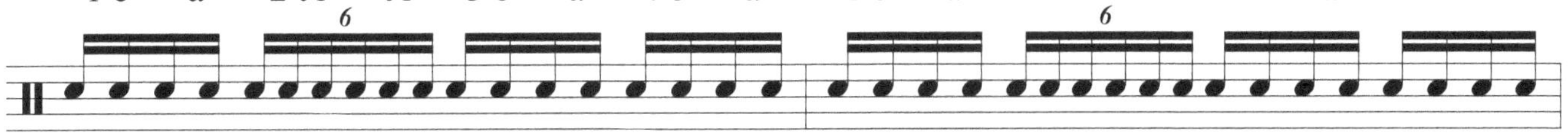

1 t l + t l   2 e + a   3 e + a   4 e + a   1 t l + t l   2 e + a   3 e + a   4 e + a

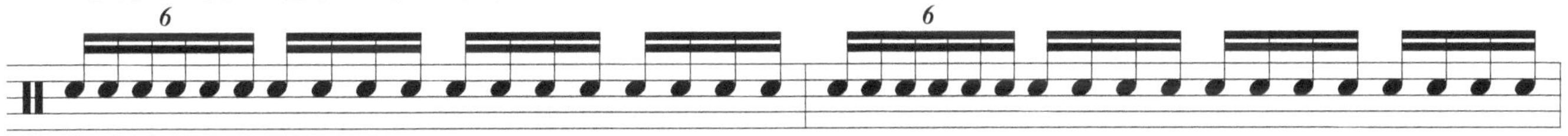

Ok guys, lets try some random variations of our new notes, without the count. Good luck!

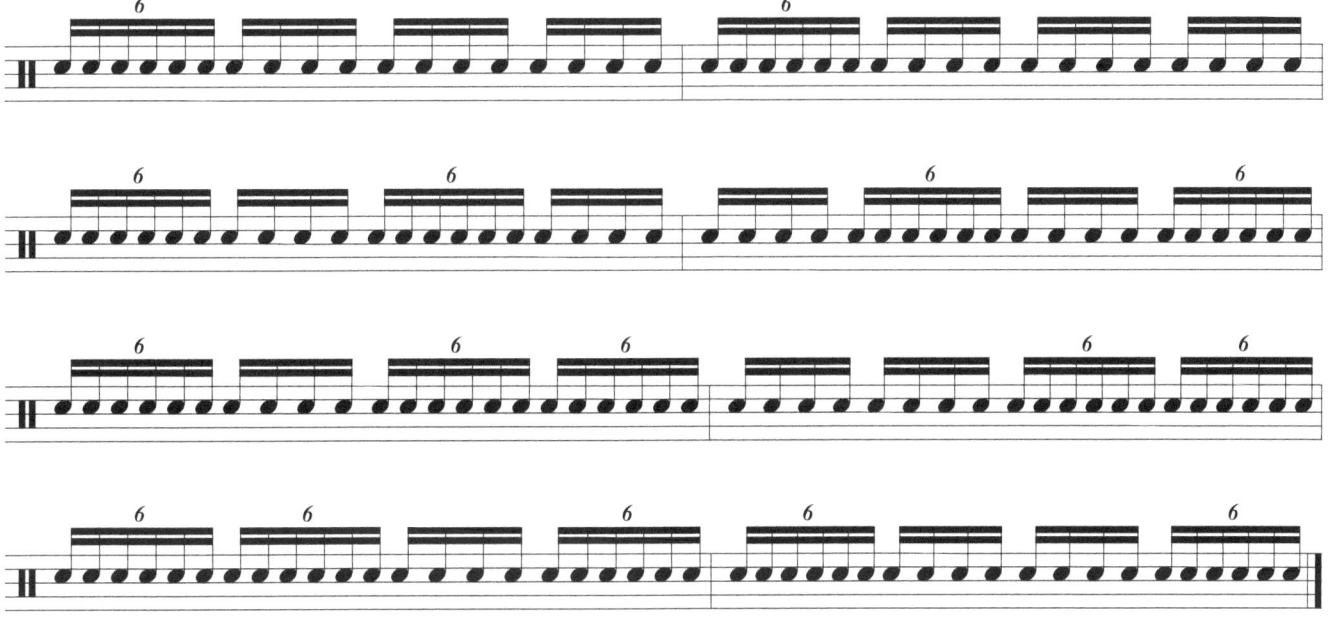

8TH NOTE TRIPLETS WITH 16TH NOTE TRIPLETS

Ok guys, here we have nothing but our irregular notes combined, remembering to allow for each triplet to last the whole duration of a qtr note in value. These triplets will feel very stretched out in time.

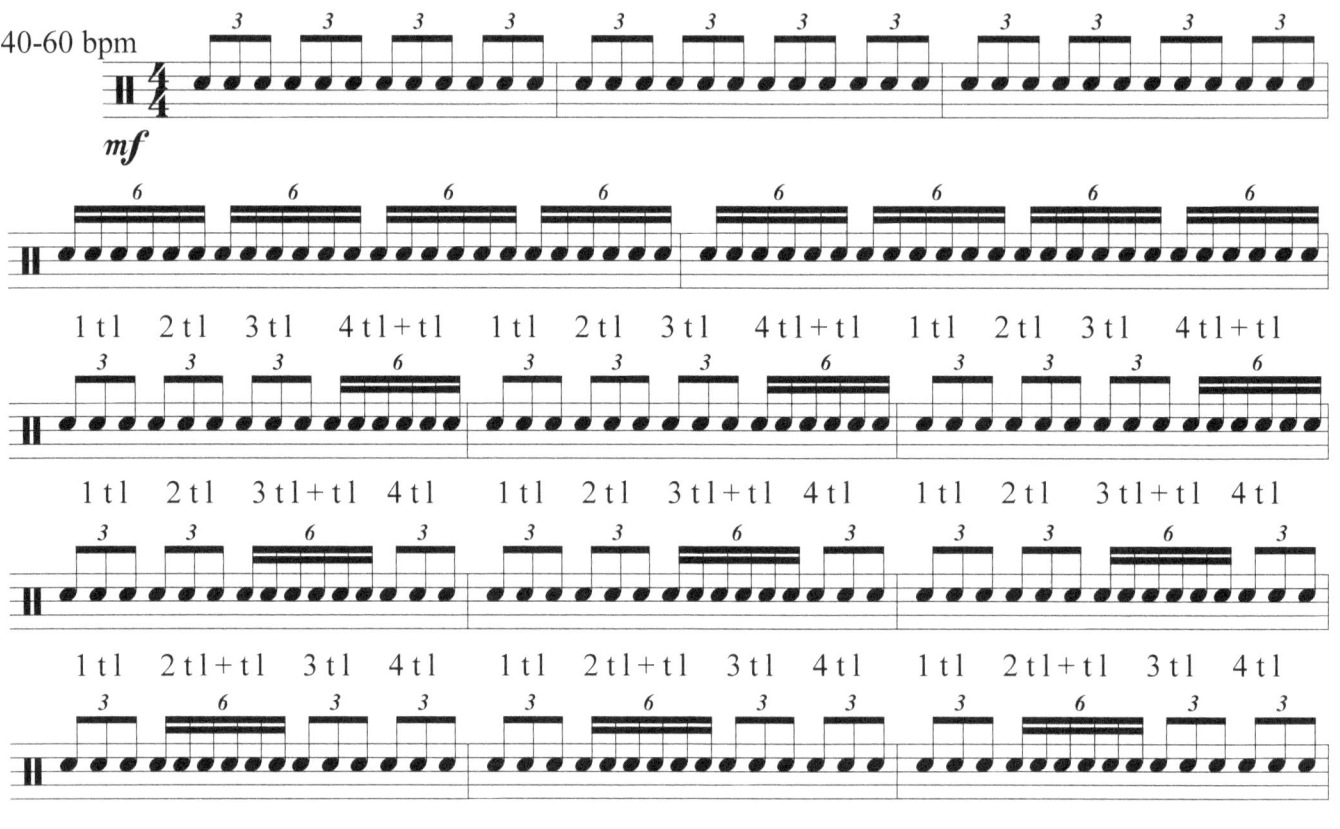

Good luck guys, lets try our triplet notation without the help of the numbers.

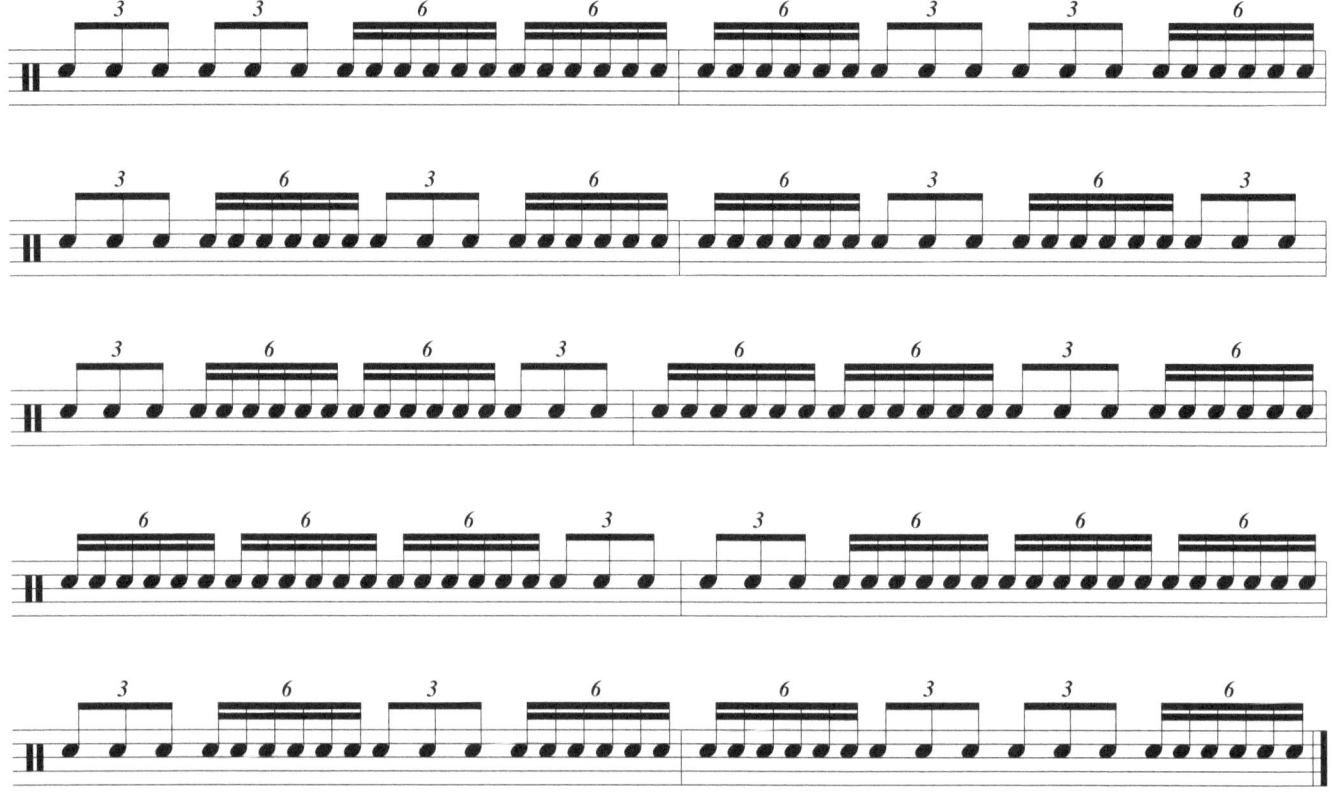

TRIPLET MIXED COMBINATION PART #1

Ok guys, here we have a two part series of mixed combinations on our snare. We have implemented our left foot on the high hat to act as our metronome, take it slow and do your best.

bpm 60-90

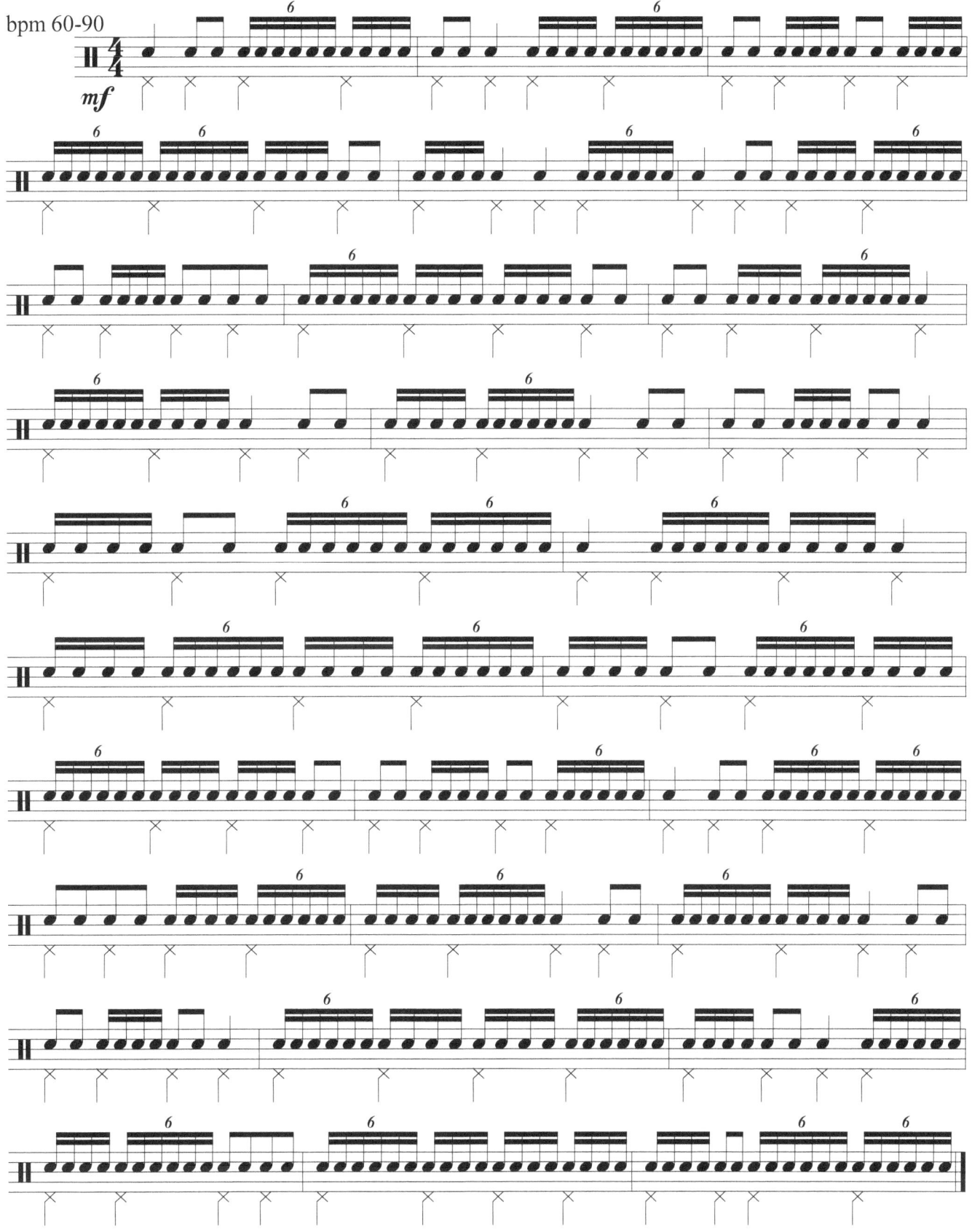

TRIPLET MIXED COMBINATIONS PART #2

Here we have part #2 using both types of our irregular notes. These are very challenging mixed note combinations, once again we have implemented our left foot on the high hat to act as our metronome, take it slow, we can always quicken our tempo as we advance through the page.

60-90 bpm

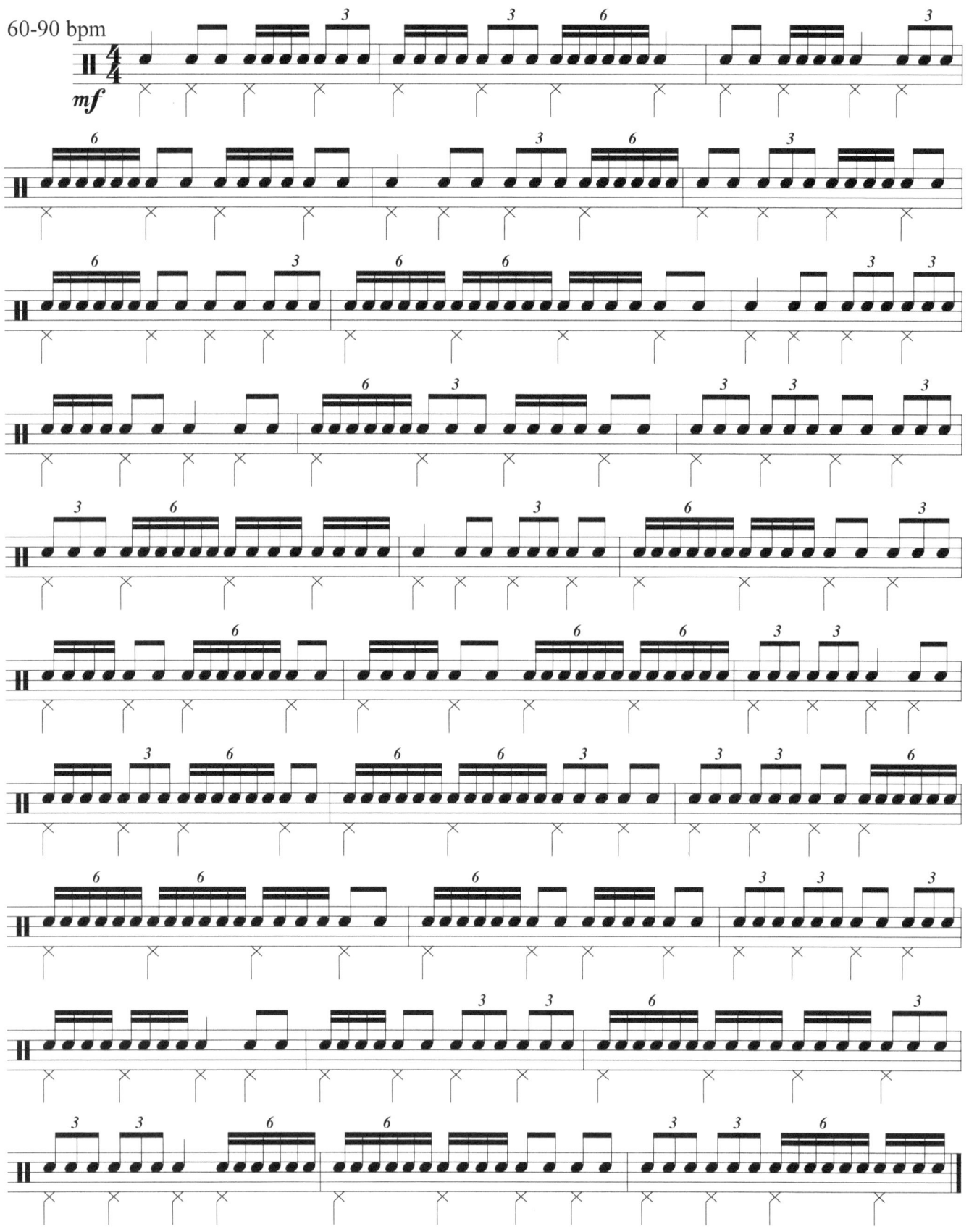

16TH NOTE TRIPLET RESTS

These are triplet rests. Just remember to count your whole groupings as 16th note triplets. These are quite difficult exercises, make sure you go slow and remember to count them thoroughly. We can always speed up our tempo as we get more comfortable over time.

Ok now lets try some random rests, enjoy!

IRREGULAR TRIPLET REST EXERCISE

This is a very challenging exercise guys, take it slow and really stretch those triplet rests out.
Once we master the triplet feel and rests, you're really on your way with your notation studies.

MIXED NOTES WITH REST

Ok guys, we have another very challenging mixed note exercise here. Be mindful of your rests and their spacings, rememeber to count out loud and go slow. Good luck!

VARIATIIONS WITH IRREGULAR TRIPLETS

Ok things are getting harder now guys, if you have come this far you have done so well on your notation. Lets take this slow and have fun, don't forget your A,B,C's.

8TH NOTE TRIPLET RHYTHMS WITH IRREGULAR ROLLS ON SNARE

Have fun with these guys, remembering the nice triplet groove, enjoy adding in our irregular rolls on the snare, you will definitely be testing your skills here. Take your time and do your best.

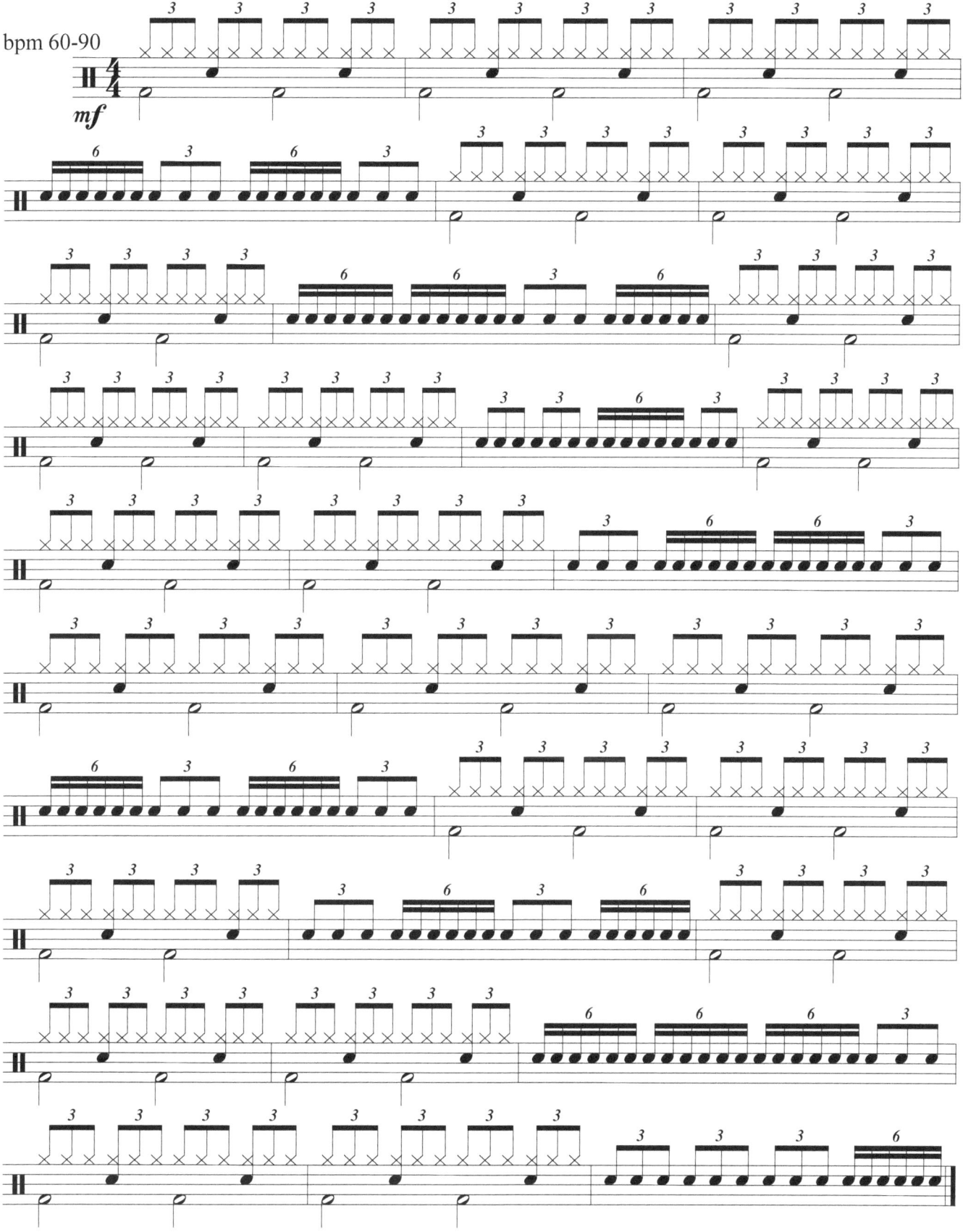

8TH NOTE TRIPLETS WITH IRREGULAR ROLLS ON TOMS

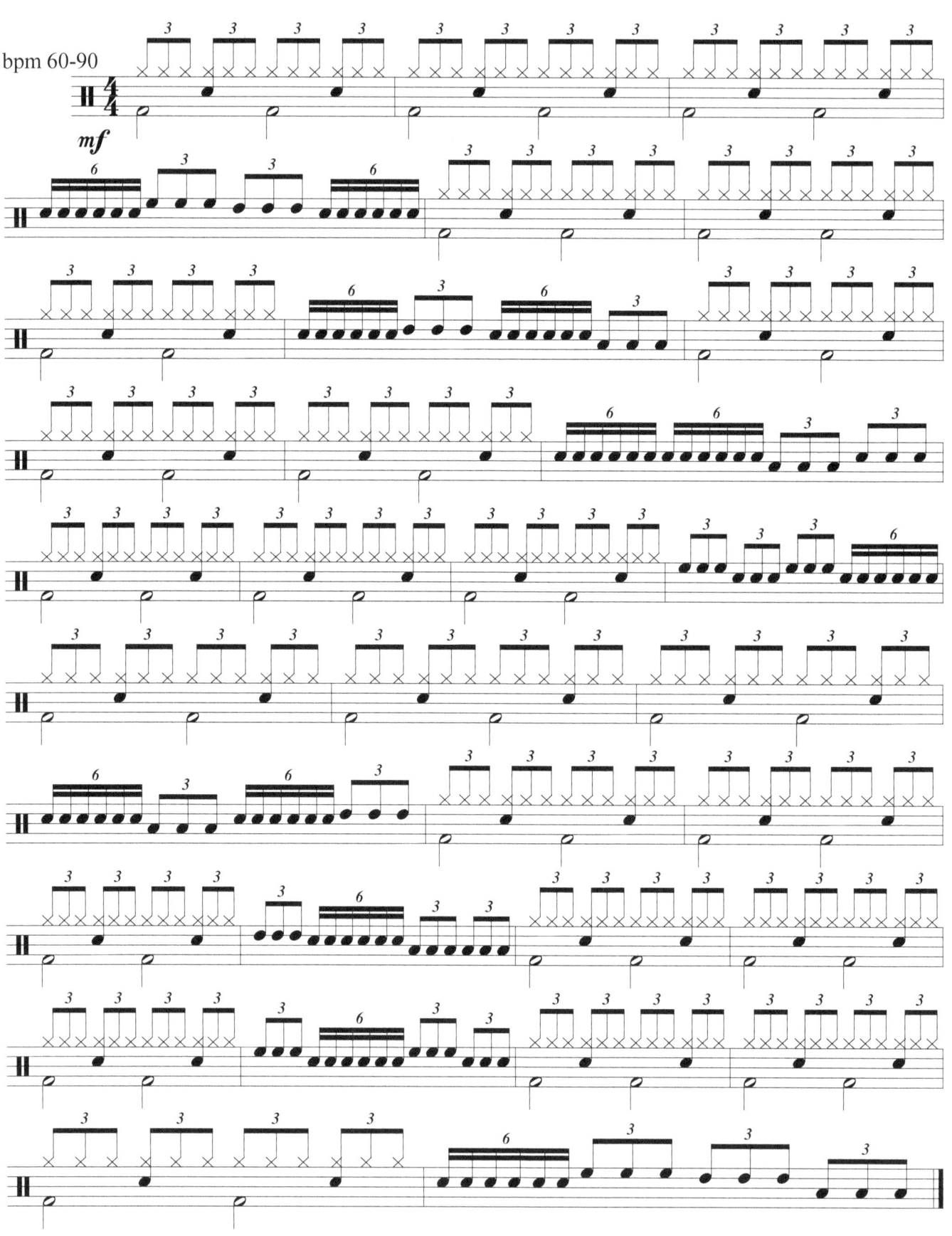

8TH NOTE TRIPLET RHYTHMS WITH IRREGULAR RESTS

Ok guys just like the previous page, these triplet grooves will get very interesting with these rested irregular rolls. Good luck!

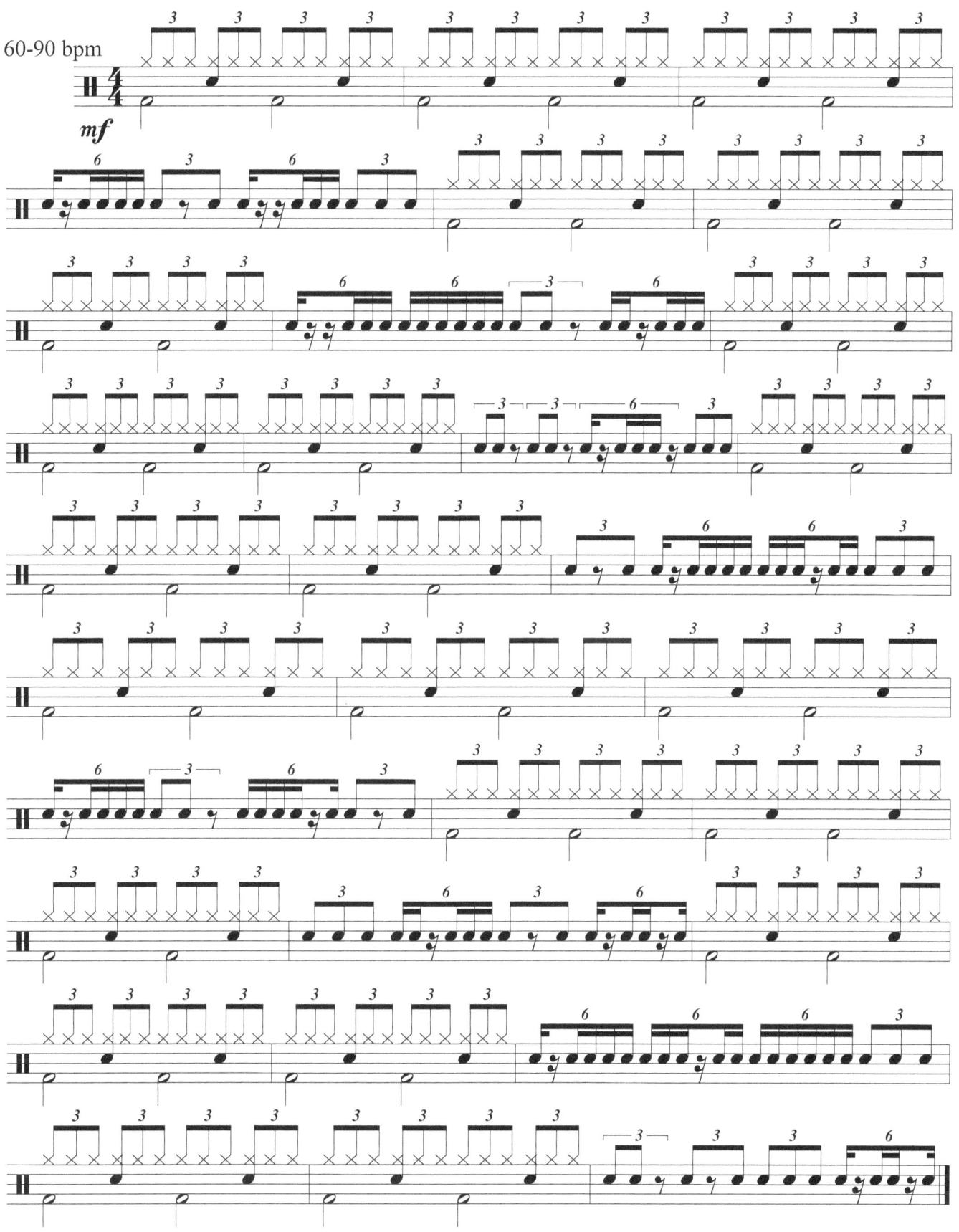

THE DRUM HUB

8TH NOTE TRIPLETS WITH IRREGULAR RESTED TOM ROLLS

Amazing job guys, you have done so well thus far understanding the irregular triplet rhythms and rolls and all the required rests that go with it. You are nearly there chapter #7 awaits you.

60-90 bpm

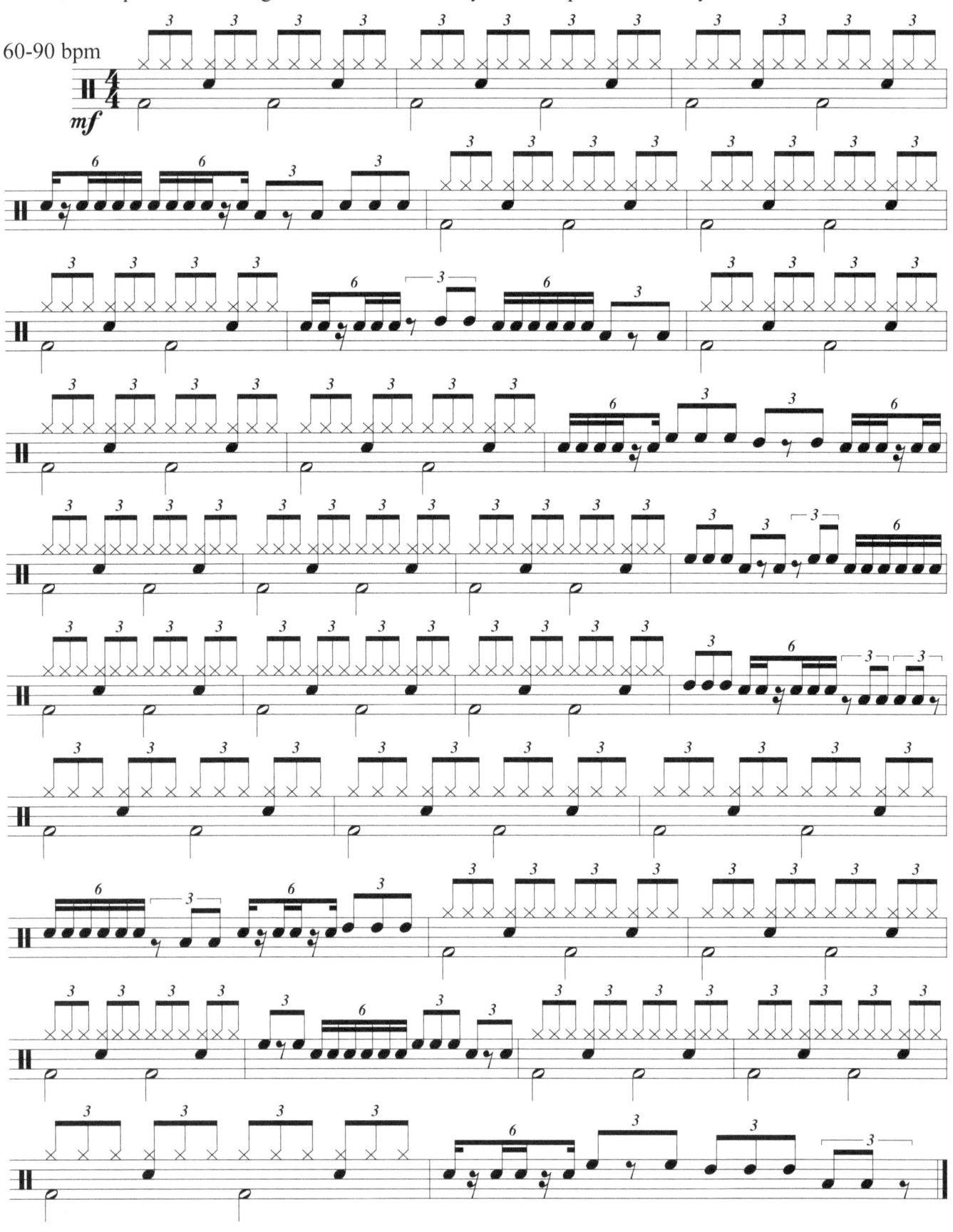

STUDENT PRACTICAL SUMMARY

On these blank staff lines use your bars to practise writing down the notation that you have learnt thus far. Try adding in your rests and write out some of your favourite rhythms. Have Fun!

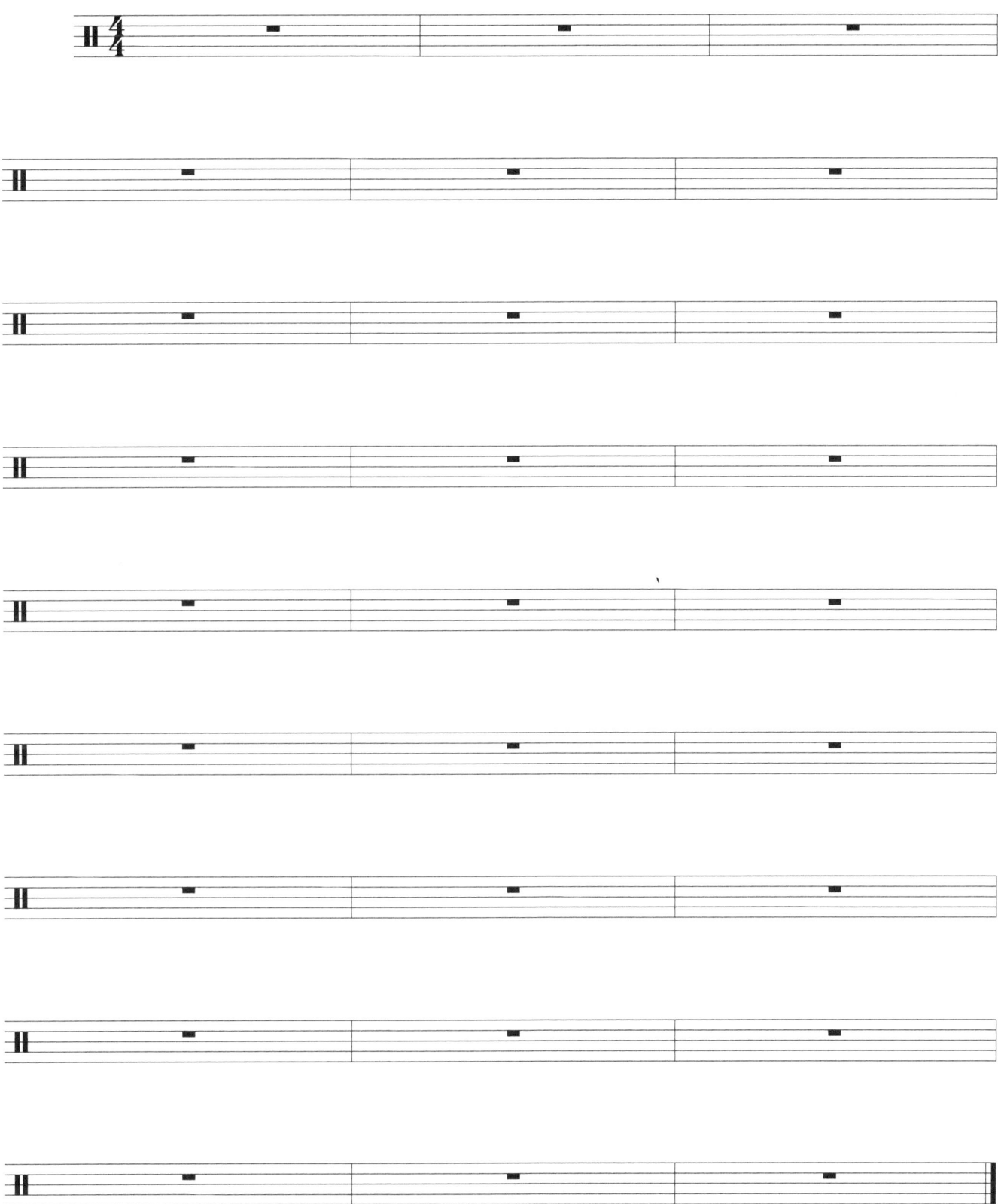

Chapter 7

32ND NOTES EXPLAINED

Congratulations, welcome to your final chapter, now we have one of our largest common note, the 32nd note, its definitely a mouthful to count out loud 1 e + a + e + a.
Just like how we count the 16th note previously in the book, we want to double that count to the 32nd note. Remembering our A,B,C's of counting, go slow and enjoy!

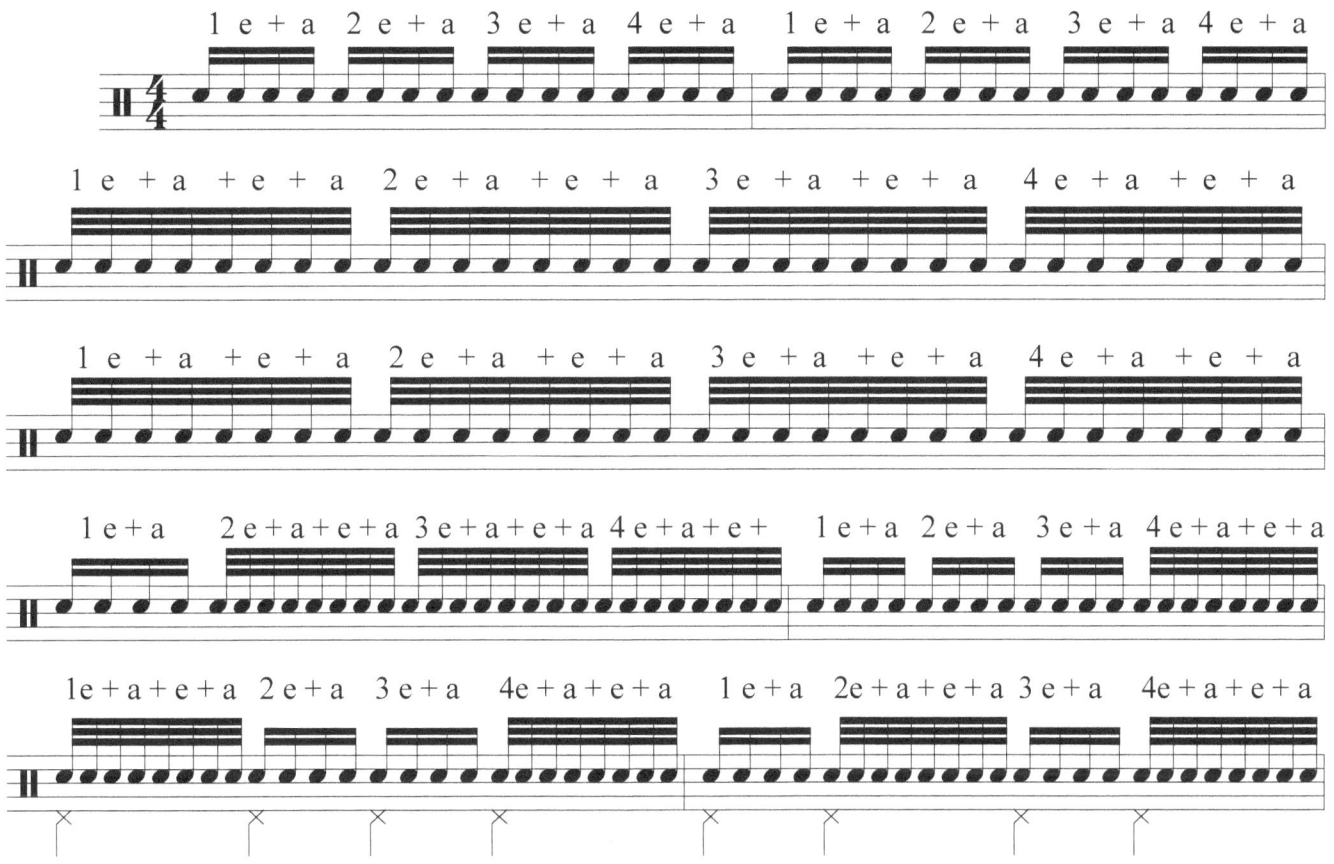

You're doing really well, lets try count our notes without the help of our numbers.

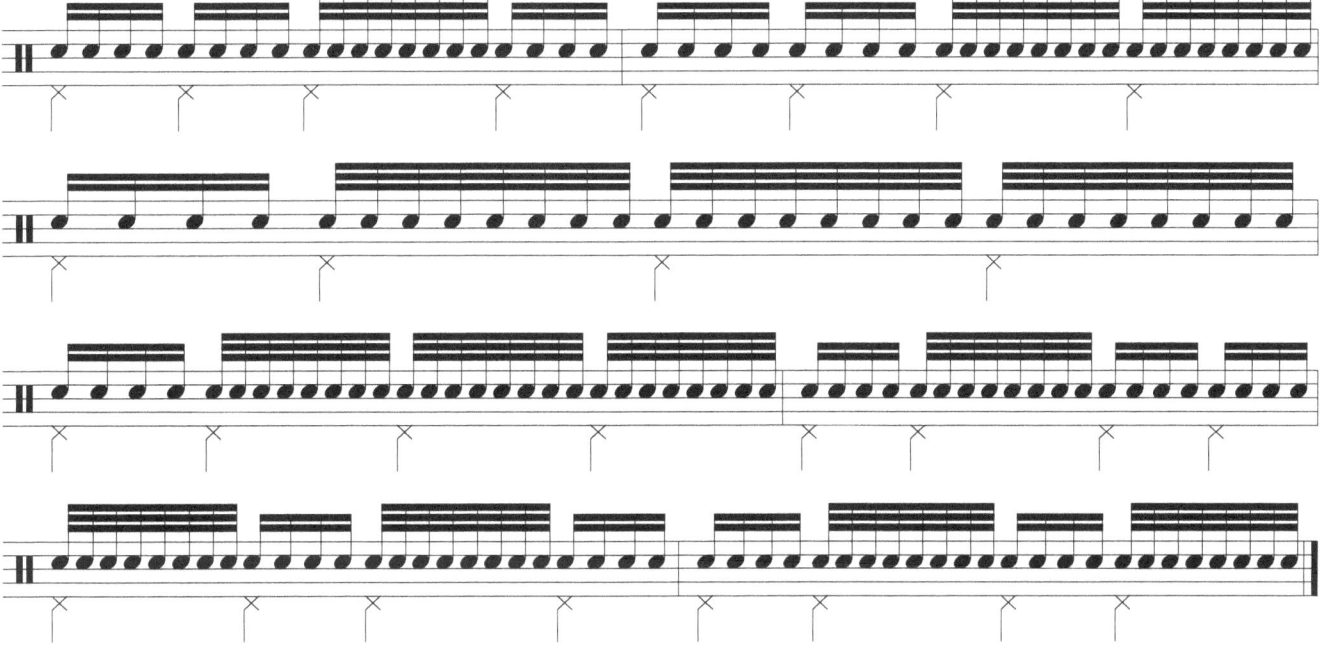

QUARTER WITH 32ND NOTES

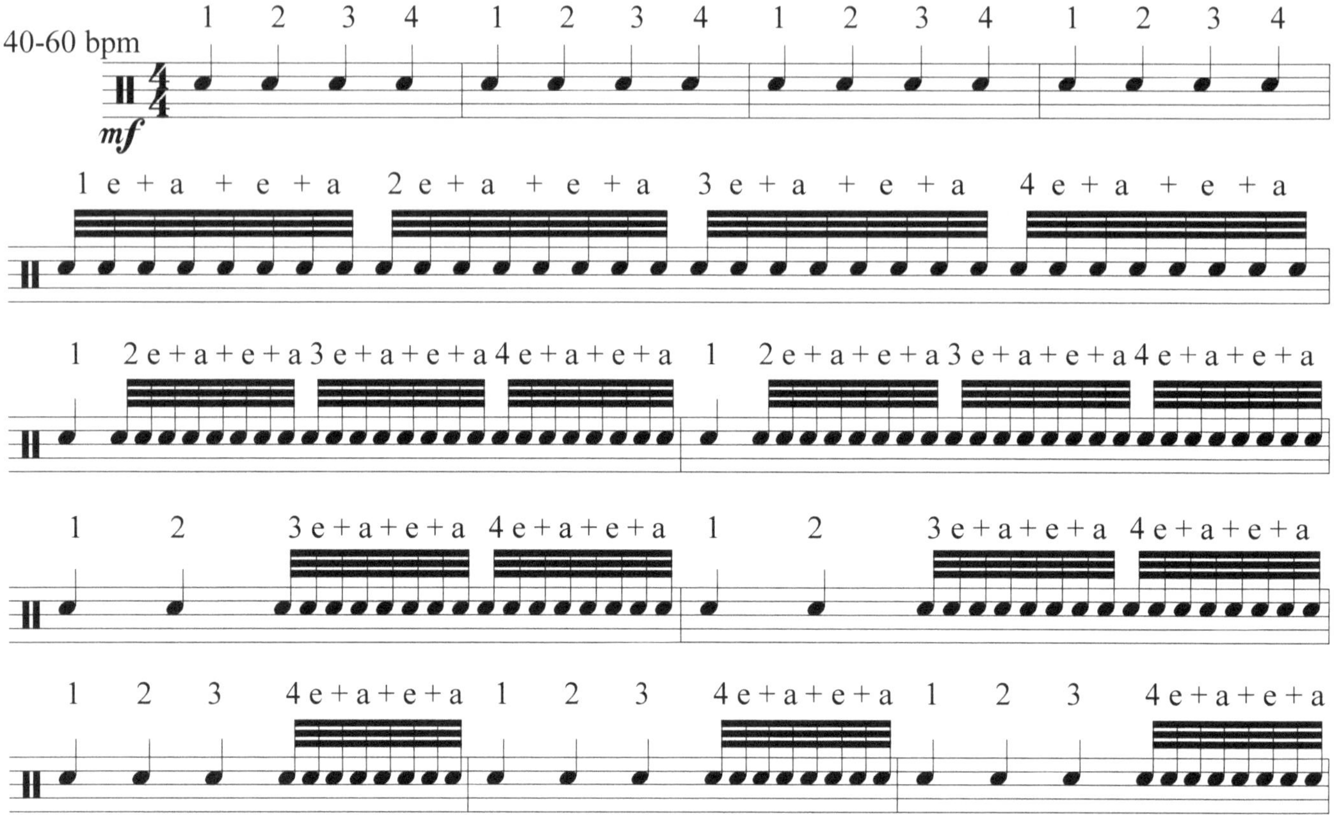

Ok lets try without the help of our numbers, good luck.

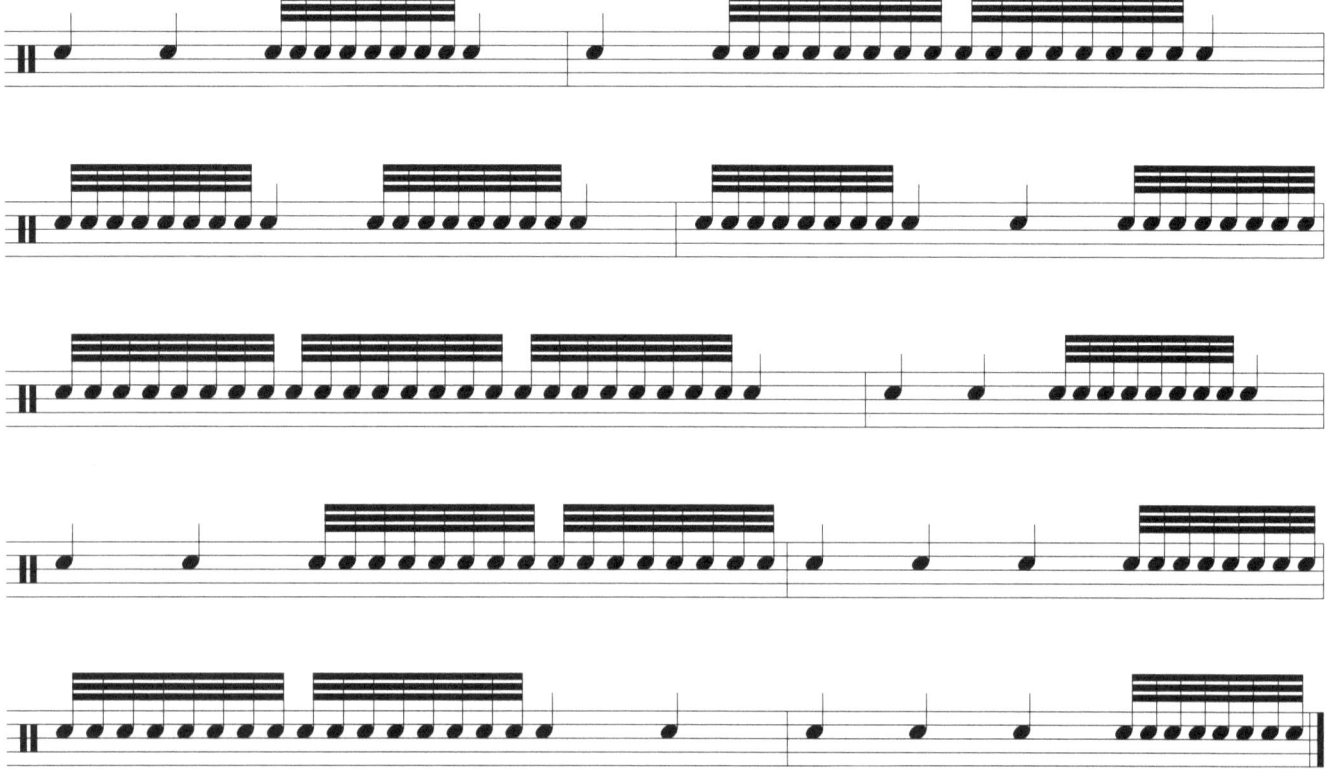

8TH NOTES WITH 32ND NOTES

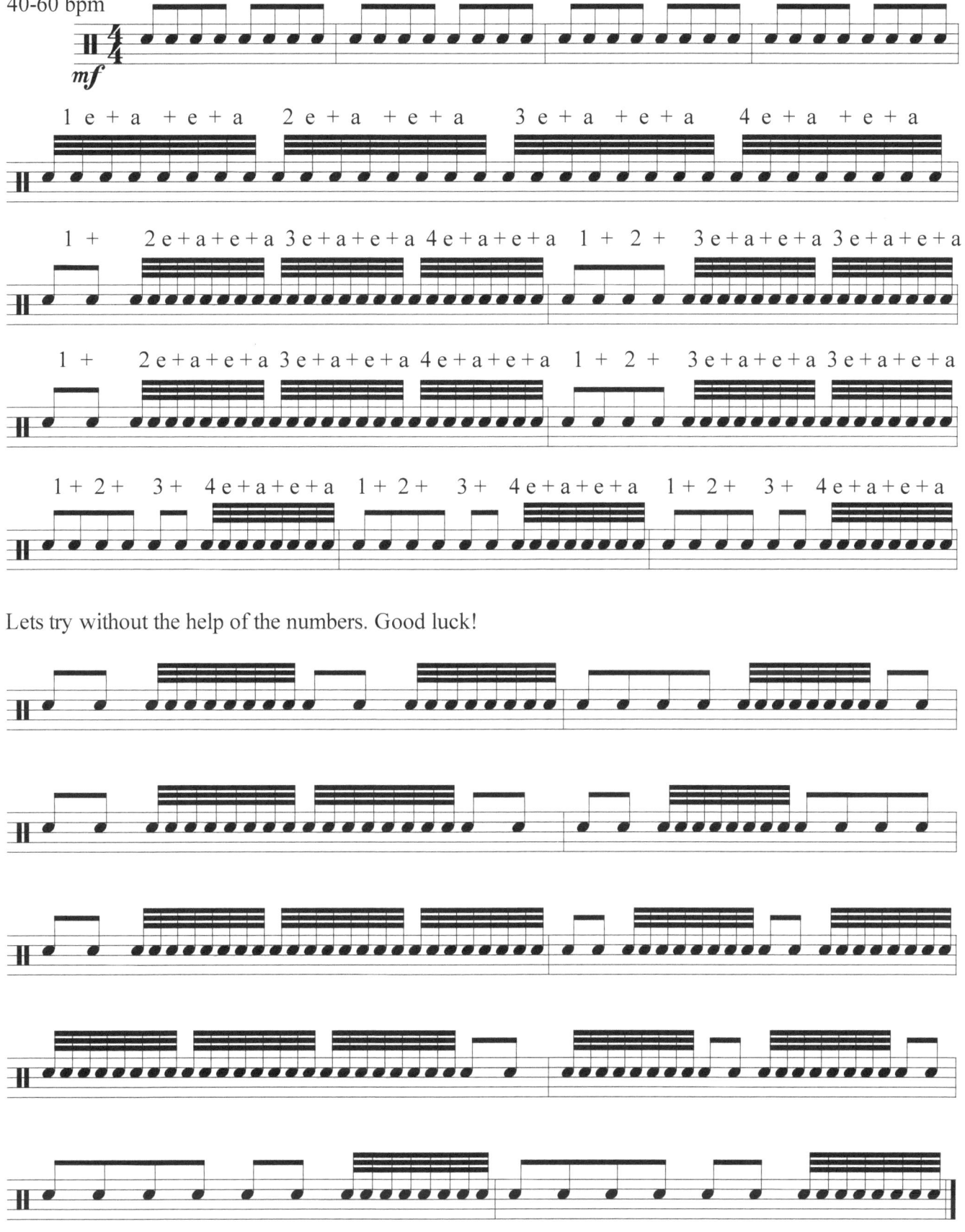

Lets try without the help of the numbers. Good luck!

BROKEN 32ND NOTES

Ok guys getting a little more complex now. What we have to keep in mind is that eight 32's go into two 8th notes, or four 32's go into one 8th note. We can also play one 8th note and not play four 32nds, we can do this at the start or end of a 32nd note grouping. Take it slow and use our mathematical jigsaw analogy.

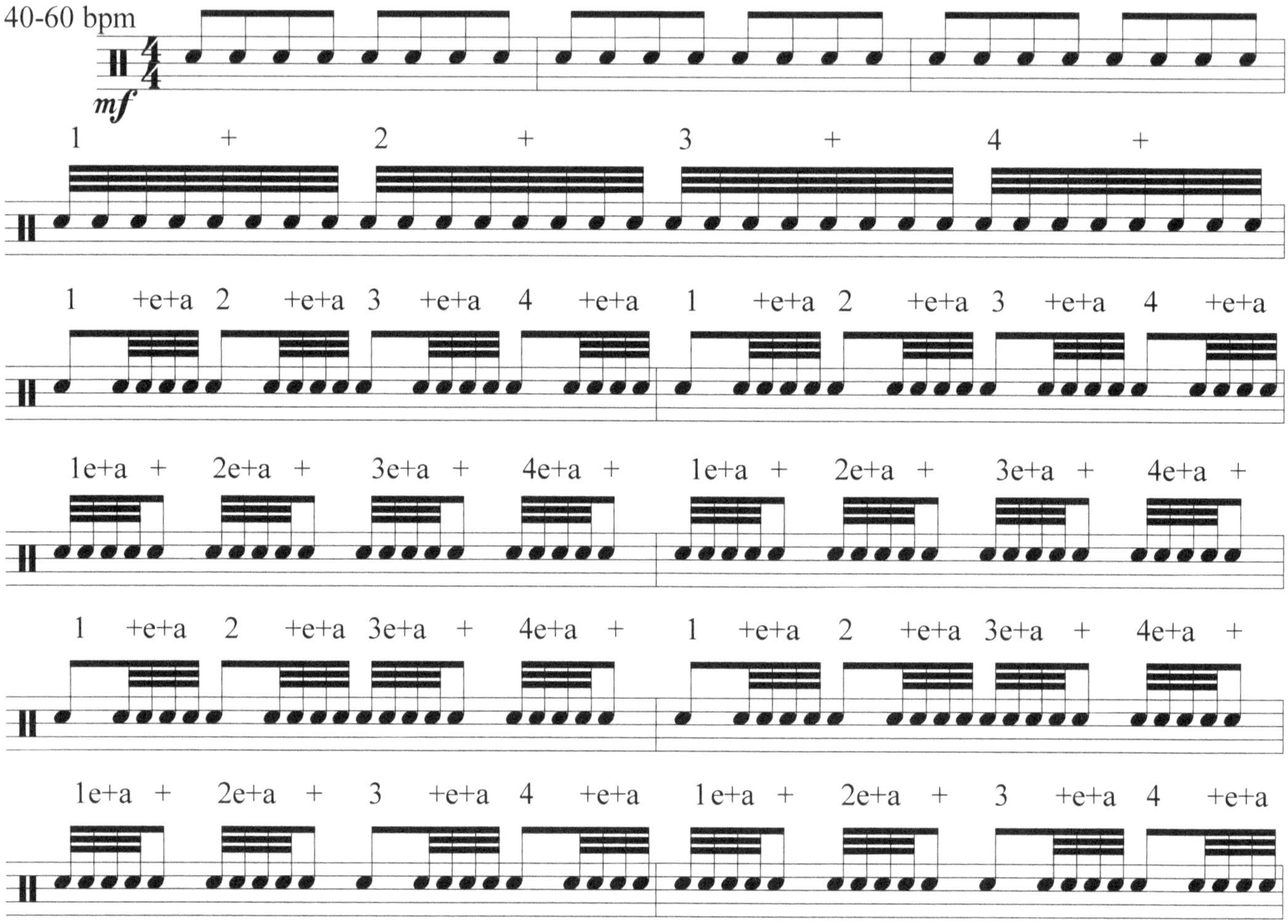

Once again guys, lets try without the help of the numbers.

16TH NOTES WITH 32ND NOTES

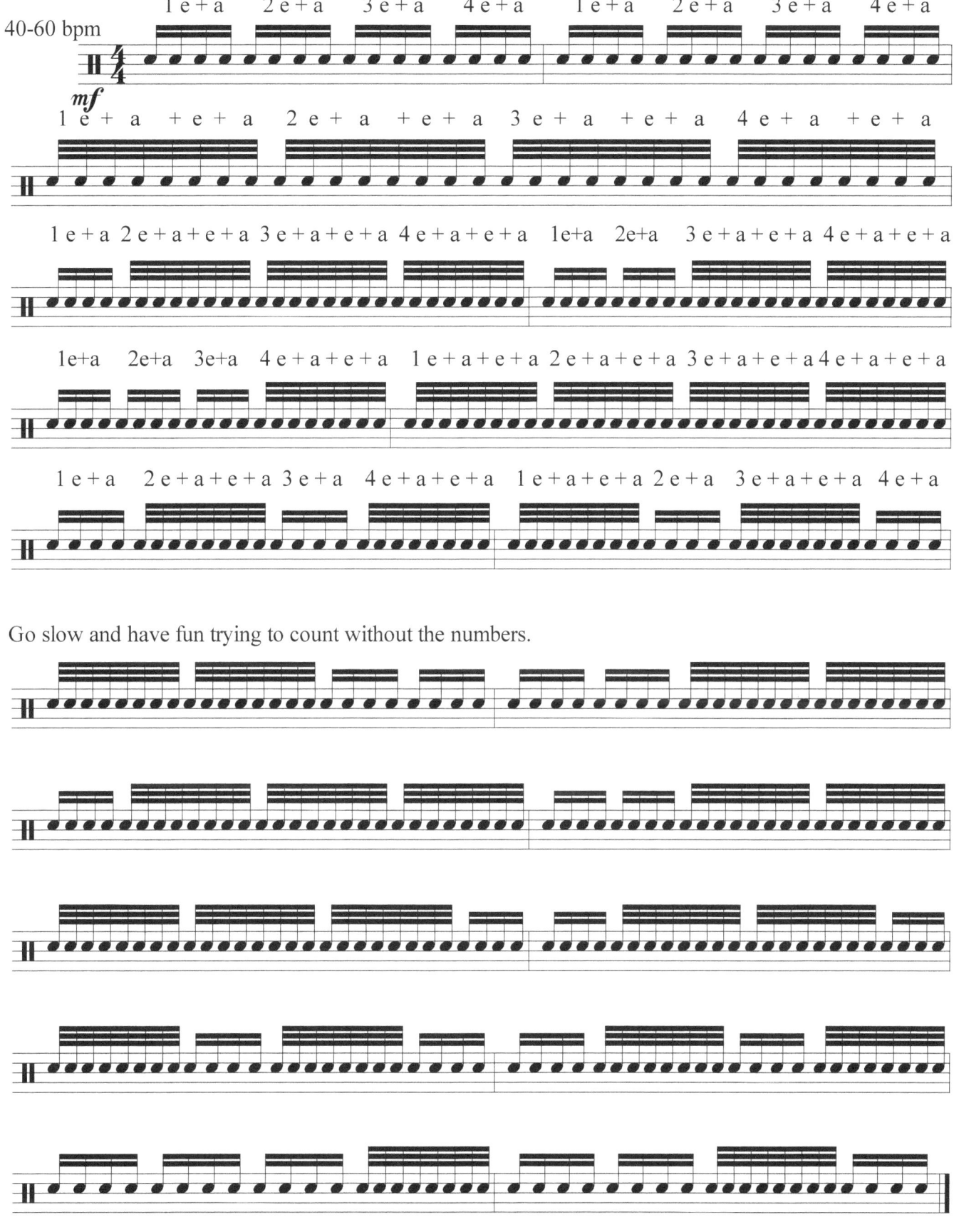

Go slow and have fun trying to count without the numbers.

RESTED 32ND NOTES ON SNARE

Wow guys, getting towards the end of the book. Just a side note, see how our 32nd note rest has 3 rest tails to match our 3 beam tails on our 32nd note. These are very important to identify which rest goes with which note. Go slow on these and follow your count. Good luck!

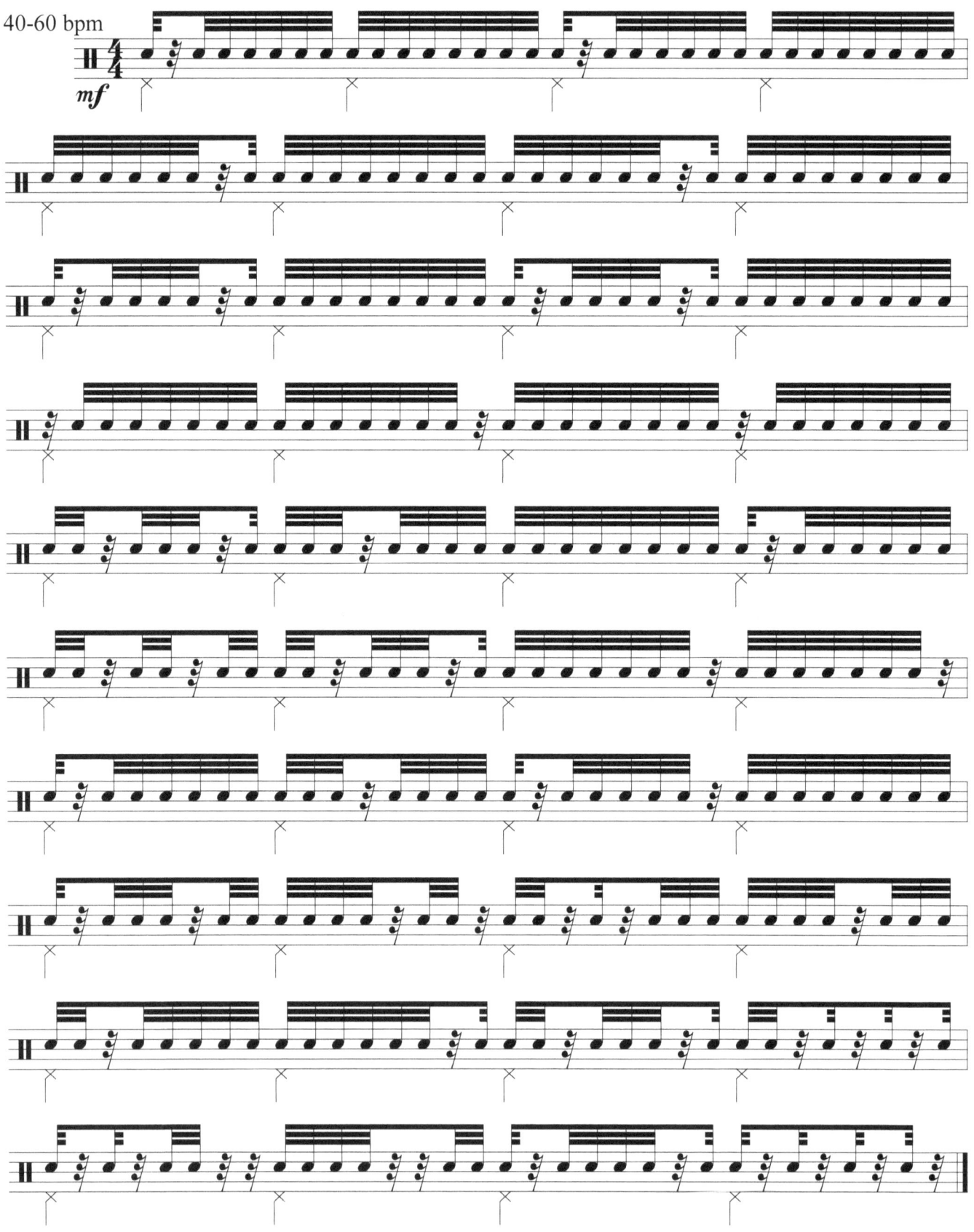

QUARTER NOTE RHYTHMS WITH 32ND NOTE ROLLS

Go slow with your qtr note rhythm tempo to start with, your 32 note rolls will come up real quick, and you might have trouble fitting them in if your tempo is to quick, think **Adagio** in terms of your dynamics.

55-80 bpm

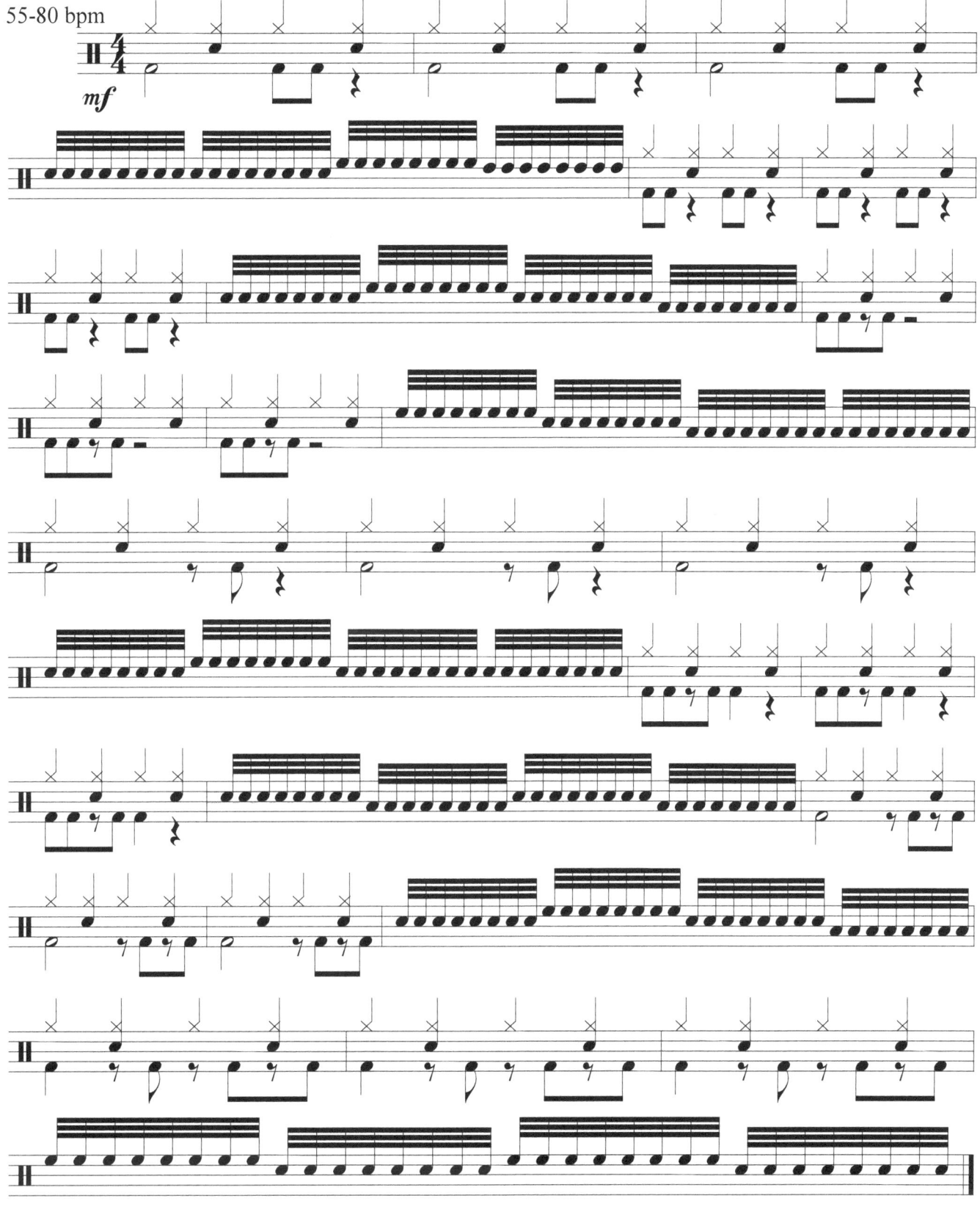

8th Note Rhythms with 32nd Note Rolls

Once again guys think of **Adagio** with your tempo marks. These are long rolls and we need to fit them in smoothly and correctly. Go slowly we can always speed up our tempo when we get more comfortable.

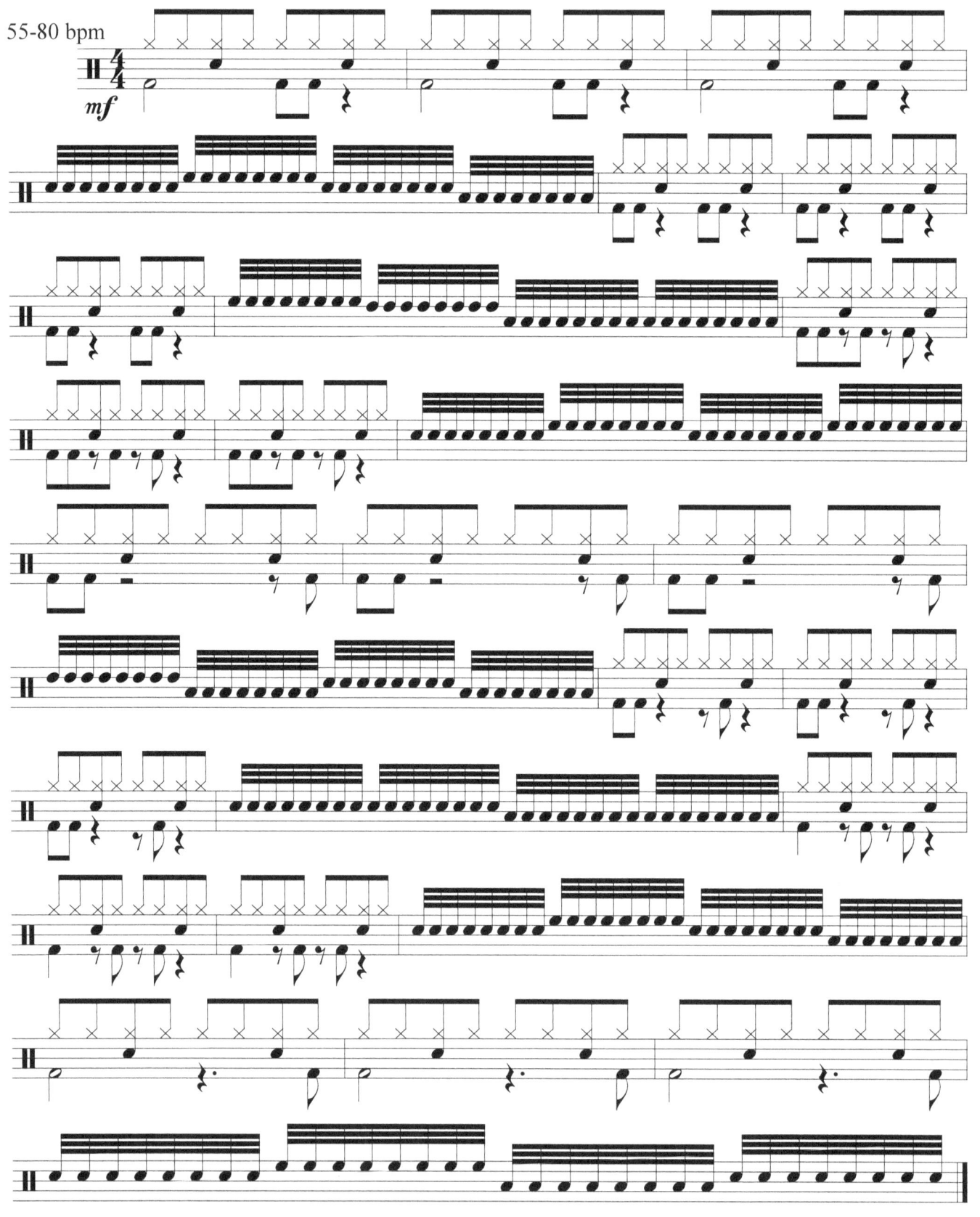

8th Note Triplet Rhythms with 32nd Note Rolls

Ok guys take your time with these irregular rhythms, because we are adding our largest mathematical note with them. They will feel awkward at first untill you get your timing right.

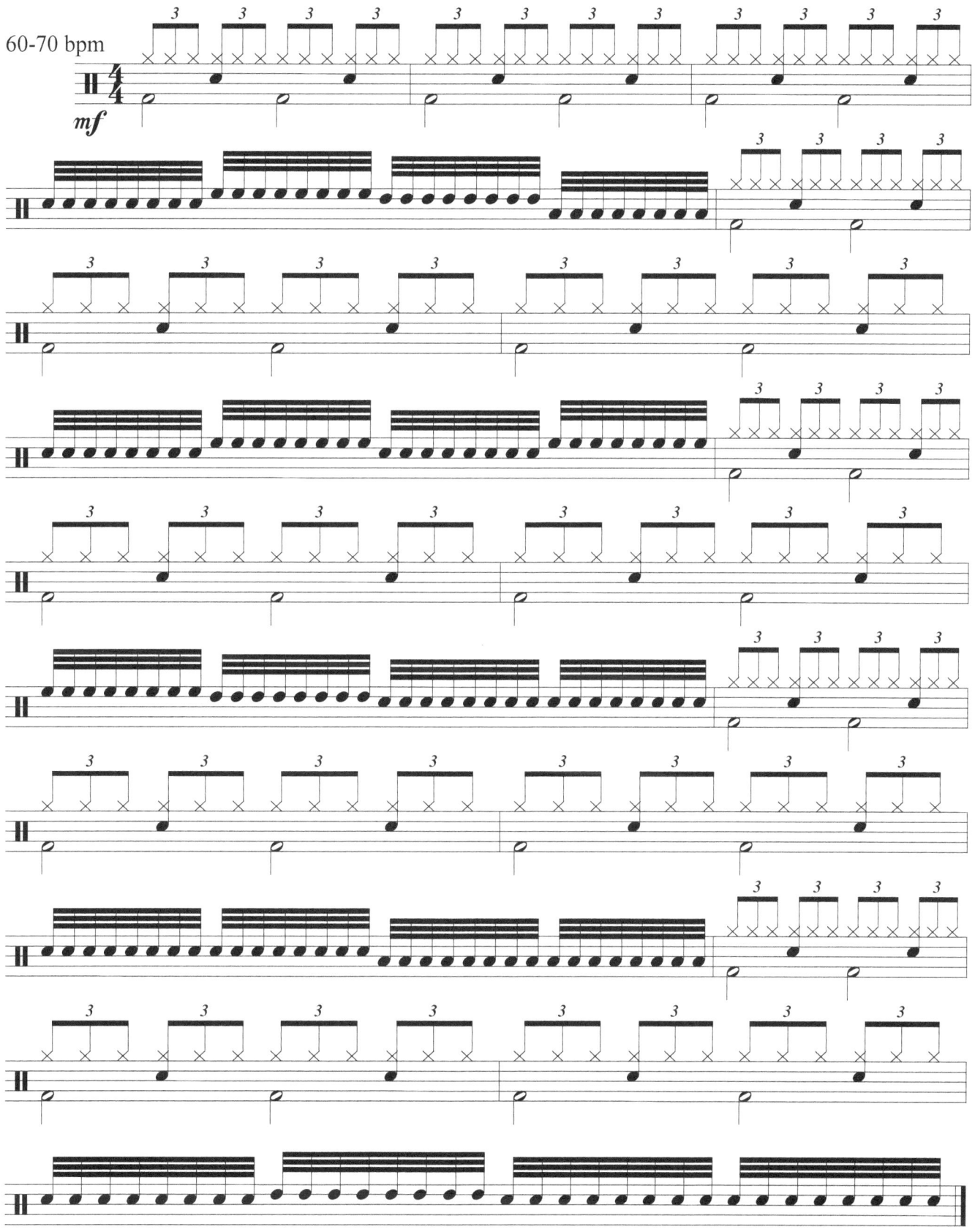

16TH NOTE RHYTHMS WITH 32ND NOTE ROLLS

Awesome work guys, you're really starting to work through your 32nd notes. Lets try our 16th note high hat rhythms, with your 32nds rolls around the toms. Go slow, we can always get quicker with these big notes once we get more fluent.

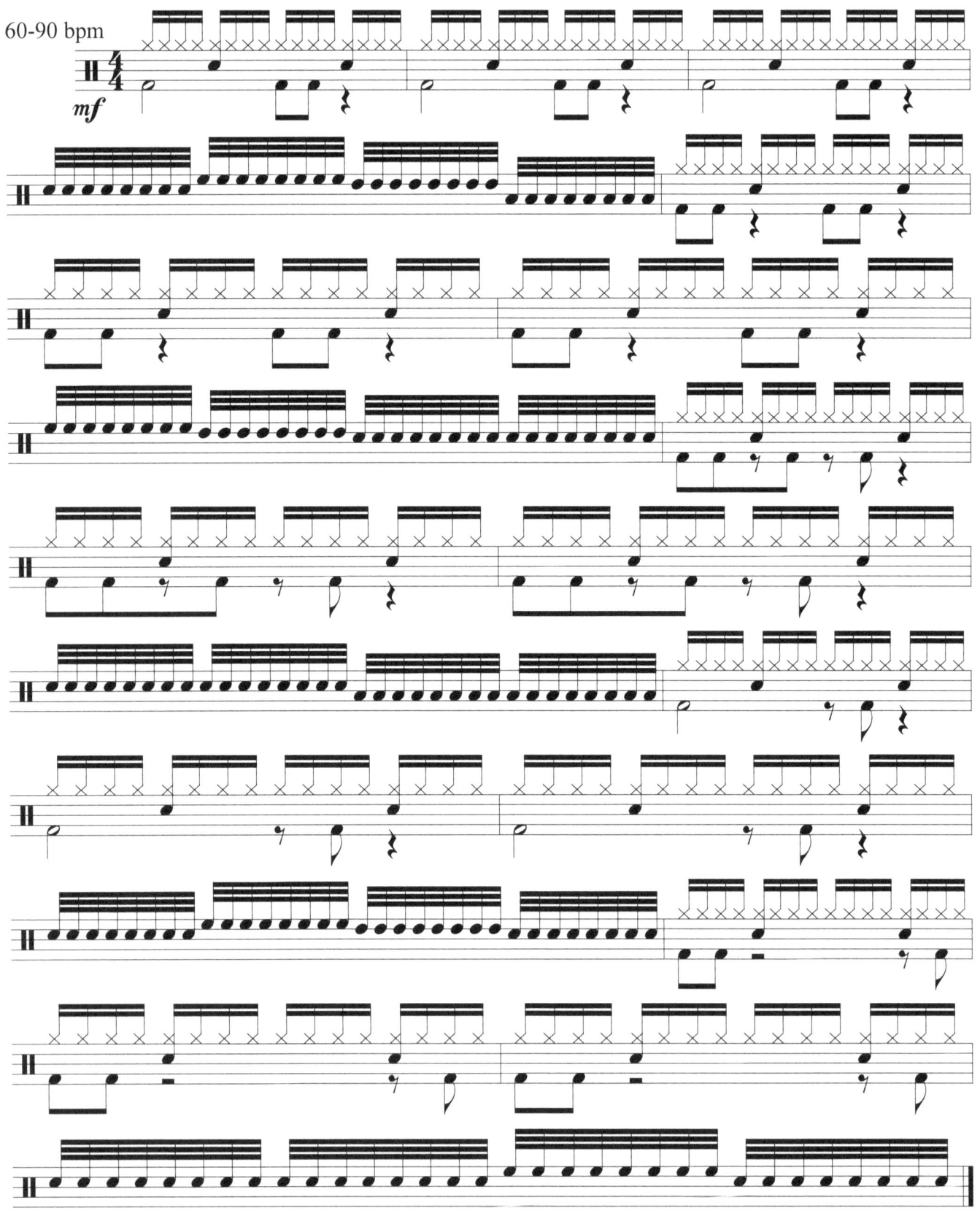

MIXED RHYTHMS WITH RESTED 32 NOTES ON SNARE

We have a bit of a skill tester here guys, with these mixed rhythms, start slow, they are very tricky. At this point in the book you have come so far with your learning of notation. You have covered so much and you're nearly there. Well done!

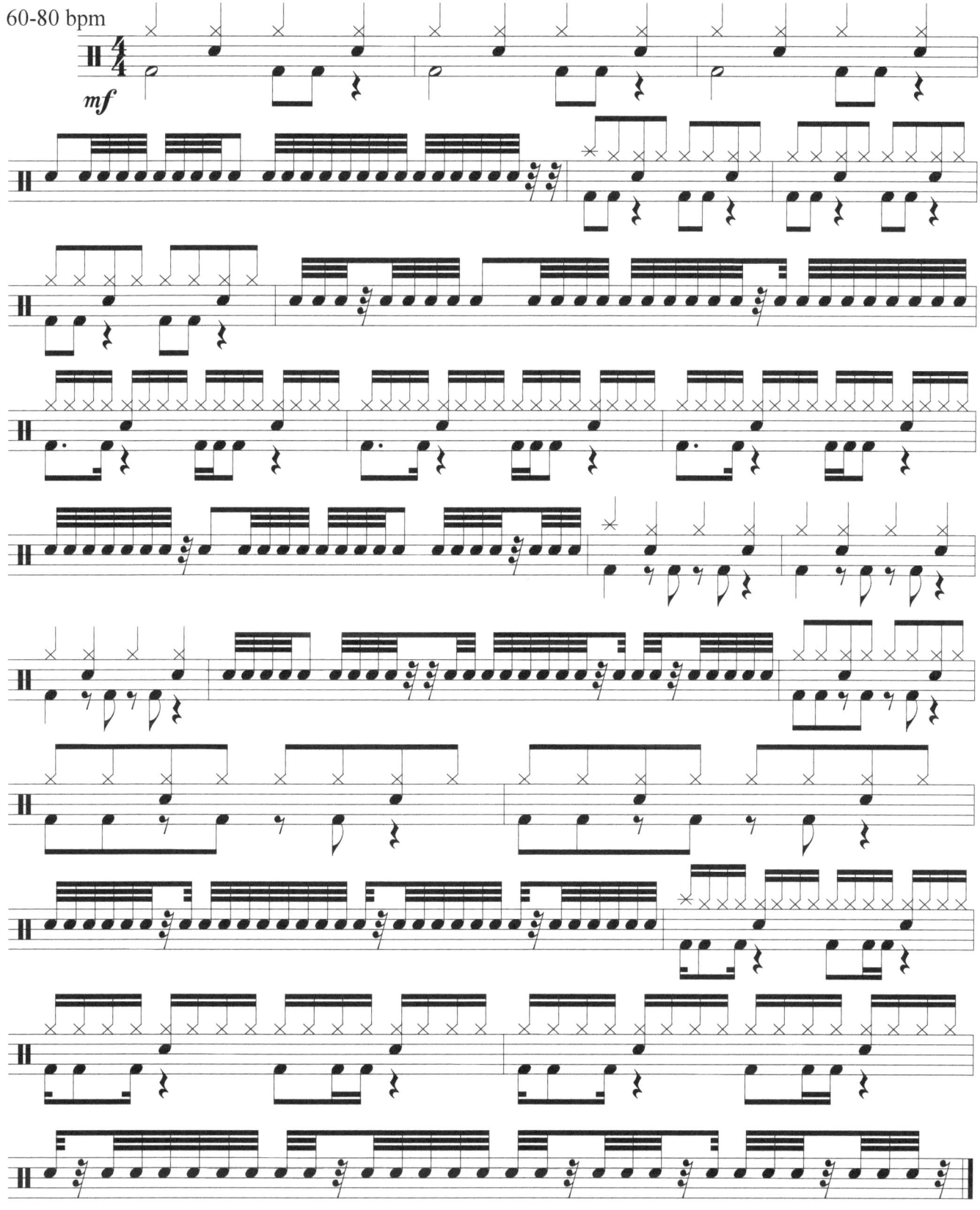

MIXED RHYTHMS WITH RESTED 32ND NOTE ROLLS ON TOMS

Just like the previous page, these are very complex rhythms guys. You know what to do.
Remember our A,B,C's. Good luck, you're doing an amazing job.

60-90 bpm

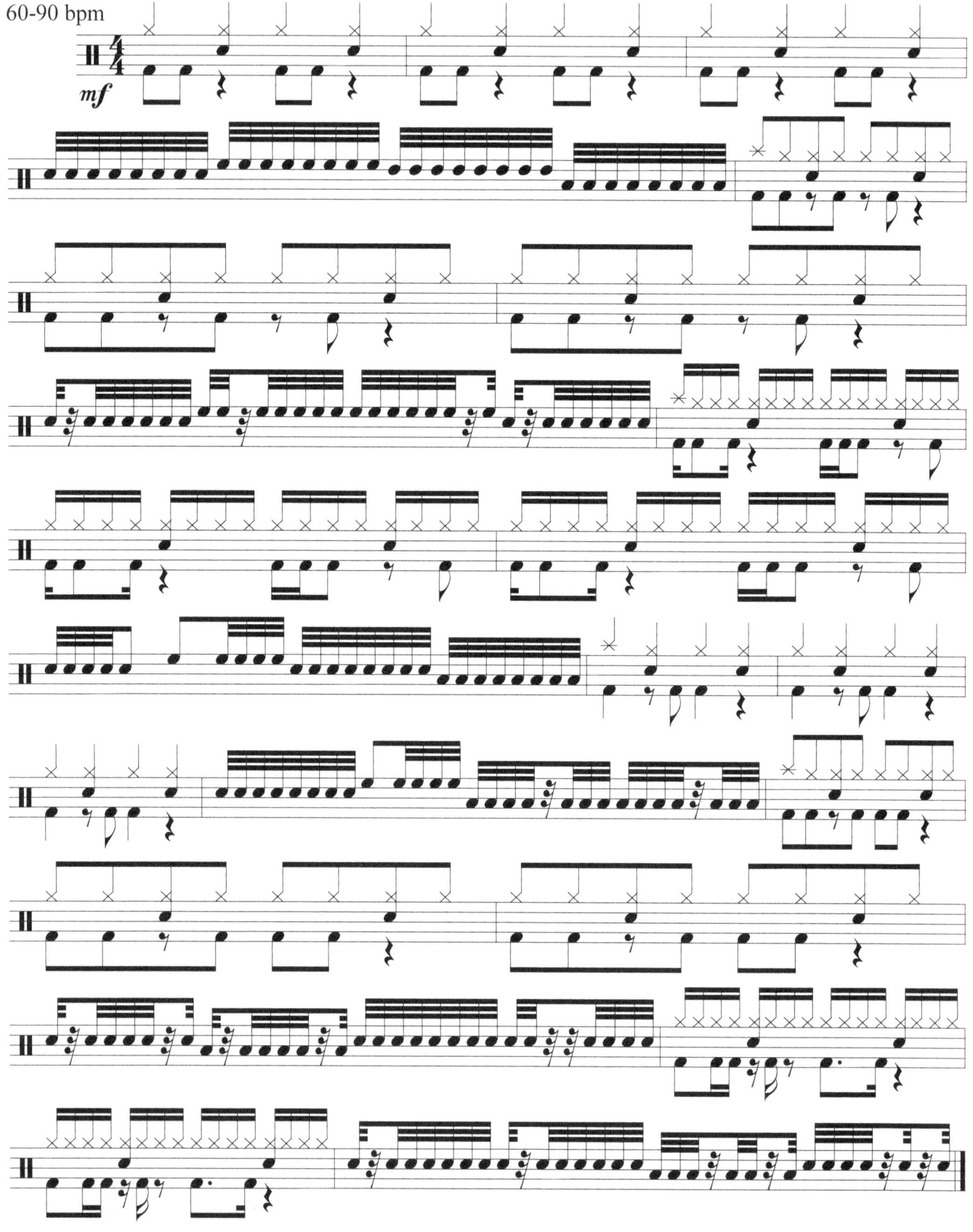

MIXED RHYTHMS WITH ALL NOTE COMBINATIONS ROLLS

Ok guys, we have all mixed rhythms now, accompanied with all of our notes we have learned thus far throughout your amazing journey through this book. Enjoy, you're nearly on your way to becoming a great drummer. Well done guys!

Whole note crash.

THE DRUM HUB

MIXED RHYTHMS WITH ALL NOTE COMBINATONS ROLLS ON TOMS

Take your time with this challenging music score. There's is a lot of information inside this music piece. Go slow guys, use all your knowledge you bhave learnt so far. You can master this sheet, you got this!

ULTIMATE MIXED NOTE COMBINATIONS PART #1

Well done guys, you have come so far with your amazing efforts and dedication towards your journey of becoming a great drummer. I hope you enjoy this next 3 part trilogy of all your combined notes and rests you have mastered thus far. A huge congratulations.

THE DRUM HUB

141

ULTIMATE MIXED NOTE COMBINATIONS WITH RESTS PART #2

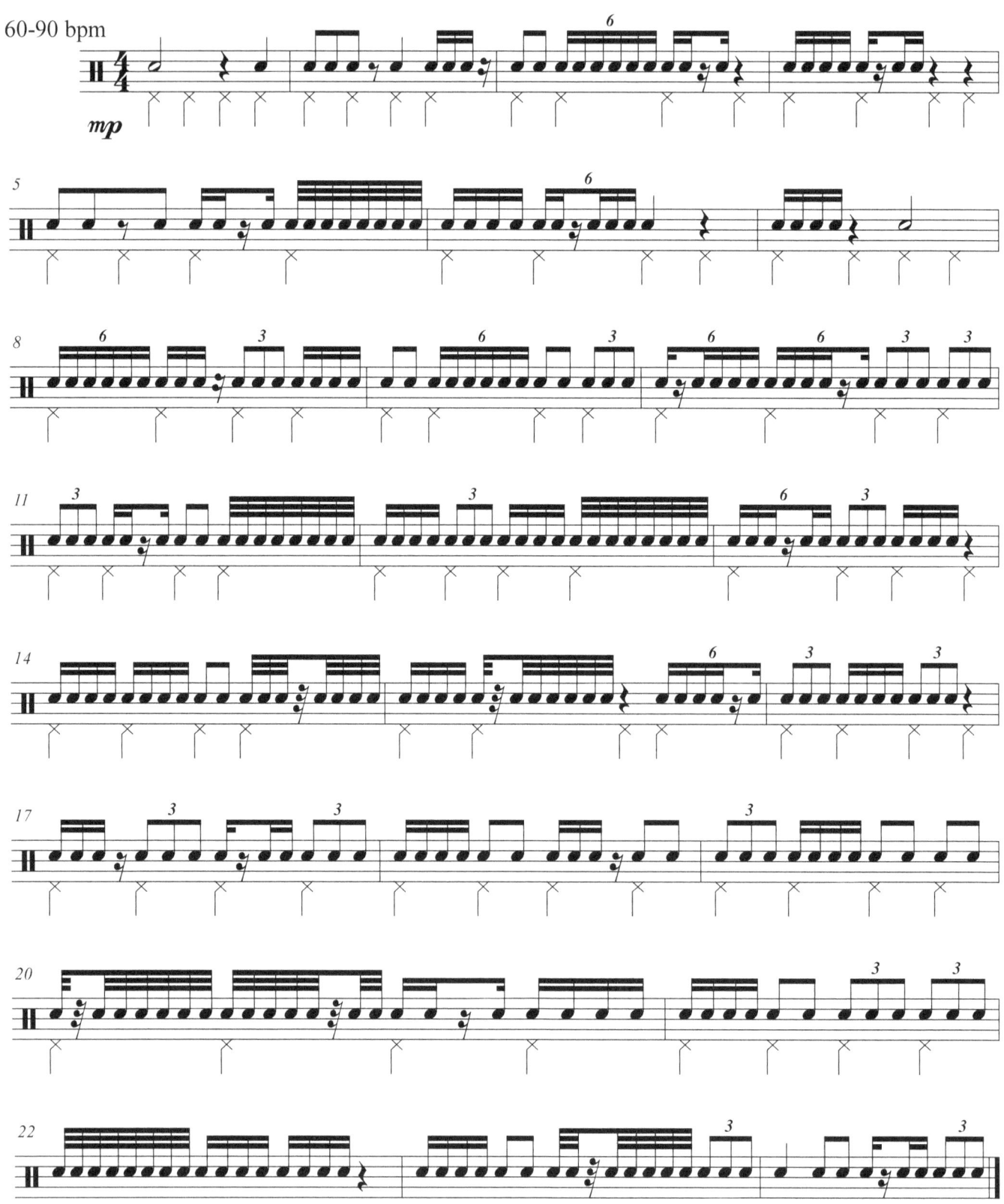

ULTIMATE MIXED NOTE COMBINATIONS WITH VARIATIONS

Congratulations guys you have done so well through your journey on the total beginner book. You have covered all your notes rests, tempo marks and dynamics. Learnt how to play rhythms and rolls, note variations and your mathematical jigsaw puzzle of note method. I hope you have really enjoyed your journey thoughout your extreme efforts following this book. Well done you should be so proud of yourself, you have done an amazing job.!

Congratulations! You have officially completed The Drum Hub Music Book! This is no small achievement—you've dedicated yourself to mastering not just the physical skills of drumming but also the essential theory, notation, and dynamic control that makes a true musician.

I know the journey wasn't always easy, but you pushed through, and now you have a solid foundation to take your drumming to the next level. Every great drummer started where you are now, and with your dedication and hard work, there's no limit to what you can achieve.

So, take a moment to celebrate this accomplishment. Keep playing, keep learning, and most of all—keep making music. Well done!

Kind regards,

Joel Hammond